Arizona Travel Guide 2023 - Beyond, With A Complete Adventure Bucket List

Hiking trails, scenic drives, road trails, shoppings, state parks, Kayaking, Hidden Gems, And More.

Dave Shaw

All rights reserved. No part of this publication may be reproduced, distributed, or transmitted in any form or by any means, including photocopying, recording, or other electronic or mechanical methods, without the prior written permission of the publisher, except in the case of brief quotations embodied in critical reviews and certain other noncommercial uses permitted by copyright law.

Copyright © Dave Shaw, 2023.

Table of Content:

Chapter 1. Introduction; Discovering Arizona: Essential Tips for a Memorable Trip

Chapter 2: Exploring Arizona: Essential Travel Tips for an Unforgettable Trip

Chapter 3: Essential Items to Pack for an Unforgettable Arizona Vacation

Chapter 4: Exploring Arizona: Transportation Tips for a Seamless Trip

Chapter 5: Navigating Domestic Travel Requirements: What You Need to Know

Chapter 6: The Climate of Arizona

Chapter 7: When to Visit Arizona

Chapter 8: Must-Visit Destinations in Arizona

Chapter 9: Top 10 Places To Visit In Arizona For An Action-Packed Vacay

Chapter 10: Exclusive Outdoor Adventures You Can Only Have in Arizona

Chapter 11: Recreational Activities In Arizona

Chapter 12: Arizona — History and Culture

Chapter 13: Best Cultural Attractions in Scottsdale and Phoenix Arizona

Chapter 14: 10 Cultural Hotspots To Visit In Arizona

Chapter 15: 45 Family-Friendly Activities To Do in Phoenix, Arizona with Kids

Chapter 16: Best Things to Do in Arizona with Kids

Chapter 17: The Hidden Gems and Secret Places of Northern Arizona

Chapter 18: Best Kept Secrets In Arizona

Chapter 19: Hidden Gems in Arizona No Family Should Miss

Chapter 20: Explore The Enchanting Petrified Forest National Park

Chapter 21: Your Arizona Packing List

Chapter 22: Best Scottsdale Resorts For Families

Chapter 23: 10 Most Famous Foods in Arizona

Chapter 24: Flagstaff Gateway to Adventure

Chapter 25: Top Things to Do in Flagstaff

Chapter 26: Top Things To See & Do On Route 66

Chapter 27: Best Backpacking Trips In Arizona

Chapter 28: Kayaking In Arizona

Chapter 29: Off-Roading In Arizona

Chapter 30: 12 Best Places to Go Shopping in Phoenix

Chapter 31: 7 National Parks And Monuments You Might Not Know About, But Should

Chapter 32: 20 Ghost Towns In Arizona

Chapter 33: Is Monument Valley Worth It?

Chapter 34: Monument Valley Guided Jeep Tours

Chapter 35: 13 Hot Springs in Arizona Where You Can Soak It All In

Chapter 36: Everything To Know About Visiting Havasu Falls in 2023

Chapter 37: 10 Best Places To Stay In Arizona On Your Trip To The Grand Canyon State

Chapter 38: Benefits of Sustainable Tourism & How to Travel Responsibly

Chapter 39: The Ultimate Arizona Road Trip Itinerary

Welcome To Arizona: A Journey of Epic Landscapes, Hidden Gems, and Wild Adventures

Welcome to the magnificent land of Arizona, where adventure awaits at every turn! As a seasoned traveler who knows Arizona like the back of my hand (well, almost), I am thrilled to be your guide to this captivating state. Get ready to embark on a journey filled with breathtaking landscapes, thrilling hikes, quirky roadside attractions, and hidden gems that will leave you in awe.

Picture this: you're standing at the edge of the Grand Canyon, peering into the vast expanse, feeling the sheer magnitude of nature's masterpiece. Your heart skips a beat as the colors of the canyon dance before your eyes, reminding you just how incredible our planet can be. And that's just the beginning.

Let's lace up our hiking boots and hit the trails. Arizona is a hiker's paradise, offering a diverse range of trails that cater to all experience levels. From the towering saguaro cacti of Saguaro National Park to the red rock wonders of Sedona, each step will unveil a new dimension of beauty.

But wait, there's more! Buckle up for scenic drives that will take your breath away. Cruise along the iconic Route 66, where nostalgia blends with kitschy roadside attractions. Wind your way through the stunning landscapes of Monument Valley, feeling like you've stepped into a classic Western movie. And don't forget to take a detour to the enchanting Apache Trail, where stunning desert vistas and pristine lakes await.

Oh, did I mention shopping? Arizona knows how to spoil you with retail therapy. From the high-end boutiques of Scottsdale to the eclectic shops of Tucson's Fourth Avenue, you'll find treasures to suit every taste. Indulge in Native American jewelry, authentic Southwestern art, and unique souvenirs that will forever remind you of your Arizona adventure.

For those seeking water-based excitement, grab a kayak and explore the shimmering blue waters of Lake Powell or the exhilarating rapids of the Salt River. Dive into Arizona's hidden oasis at Havasu Falls, where the cascading turquoise waters and vibrant red rocks create a paradise that dreams are made of.

But shh, let me tell you a secret. Arizona is bursting with hidden gems, tucked away from the crowds and waiting to be discovered. Explore the ancient cliff dwellings of Walnut Canyon, walk in the footsteps of dinosaurs at Petrified Forest National Park, or lose yourself in the enchanting slot canyons of Antelope Canyon.

So, fellow adventurers, get ready to tick off items from your bucket list, create memories that will last a lifetime, and embrace the spirit of the Wild West. Arizona is calling, and it's time to answer that call with a sense of curiosity, a dash of humor, and a willingness to explore the extraordinary.

Welcome to Arizona, where the landscapes are grand, the sunsets are painted with fiery hues, and the adventures are limitless. Let's embark on a journey that will leave you yearning for more, because once you've experienced Arizona, it will forever hold a piece of your heart.

Get ready to embrace the desert heat, witness nature's wonders, and unleash your inner explorer. Arizona is waiting to dazzle you, my fellow wanderers. Let's make memories that will make your friends green with envy and your Instagram feed the envy of all.

Are you ready? Let the adventure begin!

Sincerely,
Your Fearless Guide to Arizona

Chapter 1. Introduction; Discovering Arizona: Essential Tips for a Memorable Trip

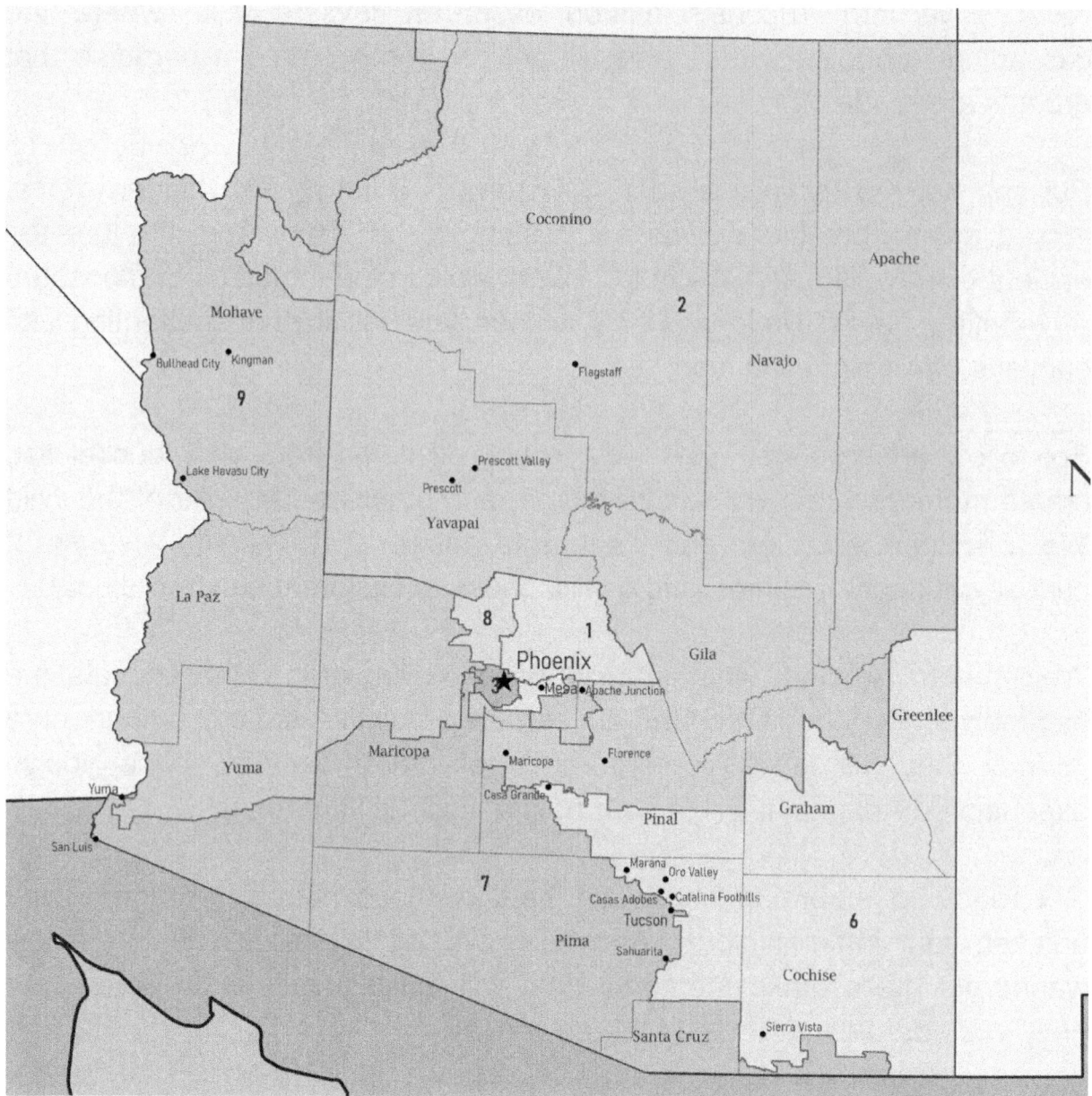

When I ventured to Arizona recently, I had no idea what to expect. I had envisioned endless sandy deserts, remote roads without gas stations, and adorable desert creatures greeting me on hikes. But reality shattered my storybook vision. Arizona has so much more to offer than just deserts, and the weather isn't always warm. Driving from Phoenix to Prescott, I was amazed by the diverse scenery that differed from my preconceived notions. I quickly realized that winter in northern Arizona feels more like the East

Coast winter. Needless to say, better preparation would have served me well. However, learning from mistakes is part of life's adventure, isn't it?

To ensure you're fully informed and well-prepared for your trip to Arizona, here are my top travel tips:

Be ready for any weather
While this tip may seem generic, it's crucial to prepare for any kind of weather in Arizona. I made the mistake of packing light layers for my trip to Prescott, assuming it wouldn't get colder than 40 degrees. But we ended up experiencing 15 inches of snow, leaving us snowed in for three days. Arizona's weather is extreme. Summers are scorching hot with the possibility of dust storms, and the fall is monsoon season. Triple-check the weather forecast before your trip and pack accordingly.

Stay aware of wildfire risks
If you plan to go camping, check for fire watches and be cautious of wildfire-prone areas. Signs along the road indicate the fire risk in specific locations (red flag warnings mean even a small campfire could cause significant damage). Take proper precautions when camping and ensure your fire is completely extinguished. Even if you're not camping, it's wise to be aware of the wildfire status in the area you're visiting.

It's not all desert
Contrary to popular belief, northern Arizona isn't entirely desert. I overlooked this fact when planning my trip to Prescott. When I think of Arizona, I imagine cacti, scorching temperatures, and abundant sunshine—not lush forests and mountains. Familiarize yourself with the specific region you'll be exploring in Arizona and consider its topography. If you're traveling north of Phoenix, expect higher elevations and lower temperatures.

Small towns may disappoint
Arizona is an outdoor enthusiast's paradise. Although I was excited to explore the charming small towns I read about, they ultimately proved to be

underwhelming. Most "Old Town" areas were filled with touristy shops and offered limited activities. Even Sedona, a popular city in the state, left me unimpressed with its downtown area. However, Sedona's hiking trails were truly amazing. My advice is to focus on Arizona's great outdoors and plan your trip accordingly. Otherwise, the journey may not be worth it.

Expect to get dirty
Regardless of the time of year, expect to get a little dirty while enjoying Arizona's stunning landscapes. Hiking in the summer can cover you in a layer of dust, while the trails can be muddy, snowy, or a mix of both throughout the year. Pack clothes that can handle sweat and are easy to clean. Opt for wrinkle-resistant garments if possible.

Car rental is essential
No matter where you stay in Arizona, having a car is essential for getting around. Distances between towns can be significant, and public transportation options are limited. Trust me, you don't want to rely solely on Uber for transportation here!

Dark sky stargazing
One of the highlights of Arizona is its designation as a Dark Sky State. This means there are regulations in place to minimize light pollution, allowing for magnificent stargazing opportunities. Make sure to visit an observatory or simply gaze at the night sky during your stay. On clear nights, you may even spot Mars, Jupiter, or Mercury (if you know where to look!).

Plan Grand Canyon trips well in advance
If you're planning to visit the Grand Canyon, even for day hikes, book your accommodations as early as possible. Lodging reservations should be made well in advance. This applies even more so if you plan to camp at the Canyon or stay at Phantom Ranch.

Stay hydrated

Regardless of the time of year, bring a reusable water bottle with you and stay hydrated throughout the day. Summers in Arizona are brutally hot, and dehydration can be a real concern. Don't rely on convenience stores being nearby to purchase water bottles. Come prepared, and you'll be grateful you did.

Explore the cultural heritage
Arizona boasts a wealth of cultural heritage sites, with Native American sites being particularly captivating. With 22 Native American tribes calling Arizona home, the state is dotted with fascinating ruins. During my trip between Prescott and Sedona, I visited sites like [specific names]—each offering a unique experience and rich historical significance. I highly recommend visiting at least one Native American site to appreciate their profound contribution to U.S. history.

By following these tips, your journey through Arizona will be even more rewarding and enjoyable. Embrace the surprises, appreciate the diverse landscapes, and make the most of your time in this captivating state.

Chapter 2: Exploring Arizona: Essential Travel Tips for an Unforgettable Trip

Arizona surpasses the storybook image of barren landscapes and deserted roads. The state, carved by the Colorado River, offers breathtaking vistas that will stay with you forever. From the majestic Grand Canyon to mesmerizing sunsets, Arizona's natural beauty is truly captivating. Feel the winter chill and admire the scenic views as you drive from Phoenix to Prescott. Moreover, Arizona offers a plethora of activities like paragliding and diving, making it an ideal destination for adventure enthusiasts.

However, like many others, you may not be familiar with the state and may feel unsure about what to expect. Therefore, before embarking on your Arizona adventure, it's essential to be well-informed and prepared. Here are some valuable Arizona travel tips to help you plan a more enjoyable and organized trip.

1. Choose the Right Time to Travel

Southern Arizona is best visited from January to March, while June to August is ideal for exploring the northern region. The state offers a wide range of attractions, including national parks, animal reserves, and sanctuaries. Consider planning visits to Tempe and Mesa during these months for an enriching experience.

2. Adjust to the Time Zone

International travelers should be aware of the significant time difference when visiting Arizona. The state follows Pacific Time Zone in summers and Mountain Standard Time in winters. Initially, you may face some difficulty adjusting your sleep pattern, but your body will adapt over time.

3. Select Accommodations Wisely

Prioritize sorting your accommodations when traveling to any destination. Arizona offers a variety of Hilton and Marriott hotels throughout the state. Luxurious resorts and hotels can also be found in nearby areas, depending on your preferences. If you desire an outdoor experience, camping is an excellent option with numerous campsites available. Whether you choose lavish lodgings or sleeping under the stars, Arizona has it all.

4. Pack Appropriately

Arizona's climate is determined by temperature and precipitation levels. When traveling during summers, pack casual, comfortable, and loose-fitting clothing. Don't forget essentials such as hats, sunscreen, and sunglasses. In winter, ensure you have jackets and sweaters for cooler temperatures. If hiking is on your itinerary, pack clothes suitable for sweating that are easy to clean. These tips will enhance your holiday experience in Arizona.

5. Be Mindful of Safety

Exercise caution along the border areas, as Arizona shares proximity with Mexico. Dehydration can be a concern due to the desert landscapes, so always carry a water bottle when exploring local attractions. Hikers planning to visit the Grand Canyon should be aware of flash floods and thunderstorms. These safety measures are crucial during your trip to Arizona.

6. Stay Prepared for Unpredictable Weather

Arizona experiences extreme weather conditions, with winters being cold and summers scorching hot. Take into account the state's unpredictable weather patterns. Check the weather forecast multiple times before packing for your trip. Spring and fall months are generally pleasant, providing the perfect climate for sports and sightseeing. Pack accordingly and be prepared for any weather.

7. Choose Your Mode of Transportation

Having your own car or utilizing cabs is advisable for getting around Arizona. The towns in Arizona are often far apart, but various transportation options are available. Buses and light rails are abundant, with stops throughout the Phoenix metro area.

8. Indulge in Mexican Fusion Cuisine

Arizona is renowned for its delectable Mexican fusion dishes, blending southwestern flavors that will leave you wanting more. Street stalls offer famous nacho chips, burritos, and salads. Rusconi's American Kitchen and Pomo Pizzeria Napoletana are highly recommended dining establishments. While alcohol is prohibited in some areas of Arizona, you can find delicious lemonades at almost every corner.

9. Immerse Yourself in Local Culture

Arizona boasts a rich heritage and diverse culture, providing opportunities to experience various tribal areas and customs. With approximately 22 Native American tribes, the state offers an authentic connection with the wilderness.

10. Plan Your Grand Canyon Trip in Advance

Even for day hikes at the Grand Canyon, it is essential to book accommodations well in advance. If camping or staying at Phantom Ranch is on your agenda, make sure to plan your trip and secure your reservations early.

Arizona welcomes all types of travelers and ensures a memorable holiday. With proper planning and packing, your trip to the state will be even more delightful. If Arizona is your dream destination, start planning your visit soon and create lifelong memories while keeping these tips in mind.

Chapter 3: Essential Items to Pack for an Unforgettable Arizona Vacation

Even the most meticulously planned vacations can be disrupted by forgetting to pack the essential comforts and necessities you need. It's frustrating when the everyday items you rely on are left behind, especially when visiting a new destination like the Southwest where you may not be sure what to bring. But fret not, we have created a comprehensive list to ensure that scenario doesn't happen to you. Whether you're exploring the Grand Canyon, experiencing the beauty of Sedona's Red Rocks, or enjoying the vibrant cities of Arizona, here's everything you need to pack for your Arizona vacation.

1. Sunscreen, Sun Hat, and Sunglasses

The Arizona sun is incredibly strong, so protect yourself with a wide-brimmed hat to shield your face. Apply sunscreen with SPF 30 or higher to exposed skin, including the back of your neck. Don't forget to bring polarized sunglasses for clearer vision and sunglass straps to prevent them from getting lost while engaging in water activities.

2. Layers of Clothing

Due to the fluctuating temperatures in the Arizona desert, pack light layers for daytime and warmer attire for evenings, including a winter hat for cooler nights. Summer temperatures at the rim can reach the 80s°F during the day and drop to the 50s°F at night, while temperatures by the river at the bottom of the Grand Canyon can exceed 100°F. Be prepared with appropriate clothing and stay well-hydrated.

3. Water and Snacks

Stay properly hydrated in the desert by purchasing an ample supply of water upon arrival. It's crucial to avoid dehydration. Additionally, pack or purchase healthy snacks like granola bars, mixed nuts, dried or fresh fruit, and nut butter to keep your energy levels up during day tours and outdoor activities.

4. Chapstick and Lip Balm

Protect your lips from the Arizona sunshine by applying sunscreen and carrying quality chapstick or lip balm with SPF protection. This will prevent sunburned or windburned lips, depending on your chosen tours and adventures.

5. Hiking Boots, Gym Shoes, and Sandals

Pack comfortable flip-flops or sandals for poolside relaxation or leisurely walks through shopping centers. If you plan on hiking or taking tours, bring supportive, waterproof, and breathable hiking boots. These will allow you to explore both wet and dry trails and protect your feet from cactus needles, rocks, and potential hazards. Don't forget to pack extra pairs of socks.

6. Camera and Cellphone

Remember to bring your cellphone and charger, as well as your favorite camera, to capture the breathtaking sights of Arizona. Whether it's Antelope Canyon, Sedona, the Grand Canyon, Tombstone, or the Apache Trail, you'll want to preserve those memories.

7. Bathing Suit

Consider a bathing suit an essential item in Arizona's scorching heat. You can use it to cool down in the pool or as an additional layer under your hiking clothes.

8. Backpack or Travel Purse

For hiking, opt for a lightweight backpack that can comfortably carry medium to heavy loads. Ensure it has enough room for essentials like water and sunscreen. Alternatively, choose a travel purse with ample space.

9. Water Mister or Bandana

Stay cool while exploring by carrying a portable mister or a bandana that can be soaked in water. These will make climbing Sedona's red rocks or navigating the Apache Trail more bearable.

10. Excitement

Lastly, don't forget to bring your energy and excitement to fully enjoy the trails and streets of the Southwest!

By packing these essential items, you'll be well-prepared for an incredible Arizona adventure.

Chapter 4: Exploring Arizona: Transportation Tips for a Seamless Trip

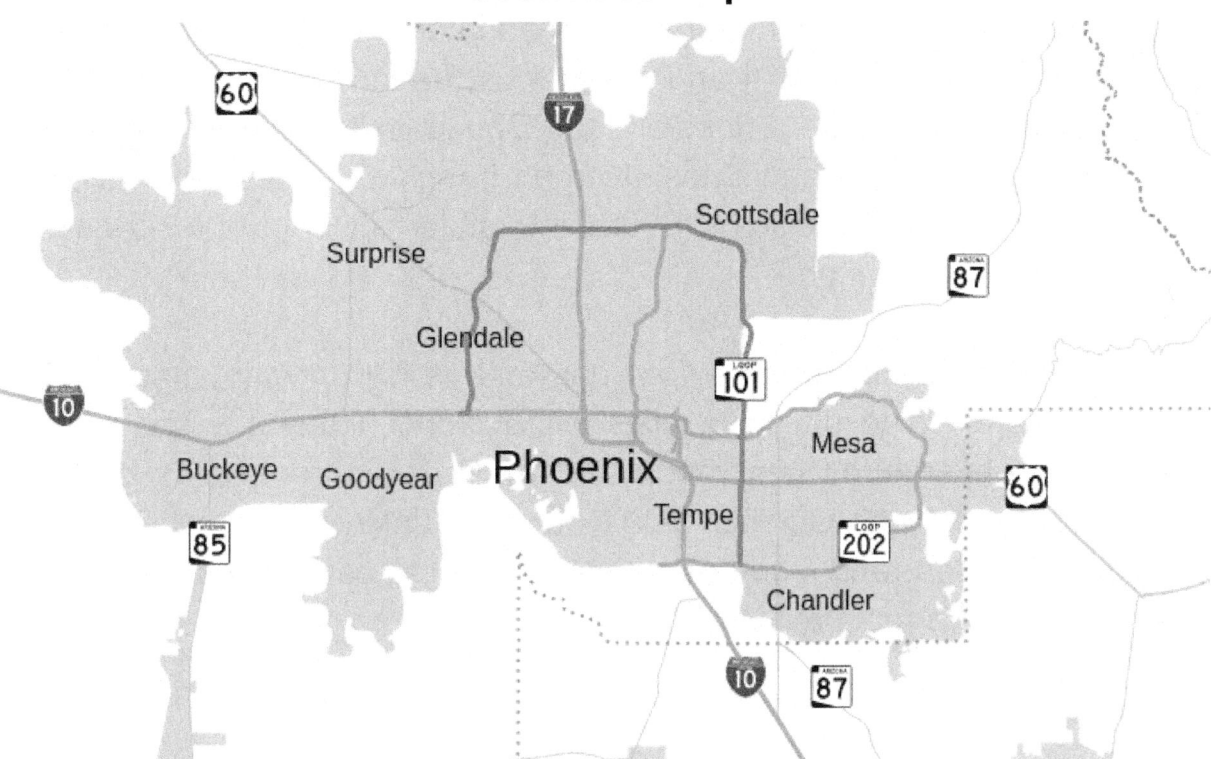

Arizona, being a vast state with top attractions mainly consisting of national parks, monuments, and natural areas, often requires a car for optimal exploration. Car rental fees in the state can vary significantly, but they have become more reasonable in recent years, aligning with other cities in the Sun Belt. However, prices can spike during periods of car shortages and high tourist traffic.

Both Phoenix and Tucson, major resort destinations, have numerous car rental agencies. Rental rates in Tucson are generally lower than in Phoenix, and you can save even more on taxes and surcharges. Renting a car at the airport in Phoenix can add over 50% to the total cost, while in Tucson, you may pay $5 to $10 less per day. Consider renting from a non-airport location if your resort provides a shuttle service from the airport.

For those unfamiliar with car rentals, websites like www.autoslash.com apply discounts from various institutions to your bill, and www.priceline.com is a reliable option.

In Arizona, you are allowed to make a right turn on a red light after coming to a complete stop. Seat belts are mandatory for the driver and all passengers. Children aged 4 and under must be in a child car seat, while those aged 5 to 7 require a booster seat. Speed limits typically range from 25 to 40 mph in towns and cities, 15 mph in school zones, and 55 to 65 mph on highways within cities. On rural interstate highways, the speed limit can be as high as 75 mph.

If you're leaving a city, ensure your gas tank is full. In many parts of the state, it's common to drive 60 miles without encountering a gas station. Note that temperatures can reach 100 degrees Fahrenheit as early as March and as late as October. Always carry drinking water while driving through the desert, and if you plan to venture onto back roads, bring extra water for the car's radiator.

By Plane
If you have limited time, flying between cities in Arizona is a convenient option. Contour Airlines (www.contourairlines.com; tel. 888/322-6686) operates flights from Phoenix to Page, near Lake Mead, while American Airlines (www.aa.com; tel. 800/433-3200) flies from Phoenix to Flagstaff.

The most efficient and convenient way to reach Arizona is by air, with multiple international and regional airports throughout the state. Additionally, a network of major national and state highways, including interstate routes, crisscrosses the state. Amtrak provides rail connections to other parts of the US through two main routes, offering an alternative mode of transportation. While public transportation options within Arizona's major cities are improving, intercity travel options via public transportation are still somewhat limited.

Taxis and Car Rental in Arizona
Getting around within and between cities in Arizona is made easy and affordable with car rentals. Major rental companies can be found at

airports, train stations, and in large cities across the state. Metered taxis are readily available in primary cities like Phoenix, Flagstaff, Tucson, Glendale, and Yuma. However, it's worth noting that taxis can be expensive, as is the case in most US states. Reputable cab companies include AAA Yellow Cab (+1-602-454-7433) in Phoenix and Discount Cab (+1-520-388-9000) in Tucson.

Trains and Buses in Arizona
Greyhound operates intercity bus services, making stops in major metropolitan areas such as Phoenix, Tucson, Yuma, and Glendale. However, transportation between cities is relatively limited beyond Greyhound services.

Arizona's larger cities have well-organized and affordable bus networks, including the Mountain Line in Flagstaff and Phoenix's Valley Metro, which offers express bus routes. Buses are a cost-effective and reasonably comfortable option for traveling within major cities.

Greyhound (www.greyhound.com; tel. 800/321-2222) and Trailways (www.trailways.com; tel. 877/467-3346) offer bus services across the state. Arizona Shuttle (www.arizonashuttle.com) provides shuttle bus service between most tourist cities in the central part of the state.

In Phoenix, Valley Metro also manages a light rail network. Northern Arizona is served by the Amtrak Southwest Chief route, connecting Chicago to Los Angeles, while the south-central region is covered by the Sunset Limited track, running from New Orleans to Los Angeles. However, it's important to note that roads are generally more prevalent and practical for transportation in Arizona compared to train lines.

With these transportation tips in mind, you'll be well-prepared to explore the beauty of Arizona with ease and convenience.

Chapter 5: Navigating Domestic Travel Requirements: What You Need to Know

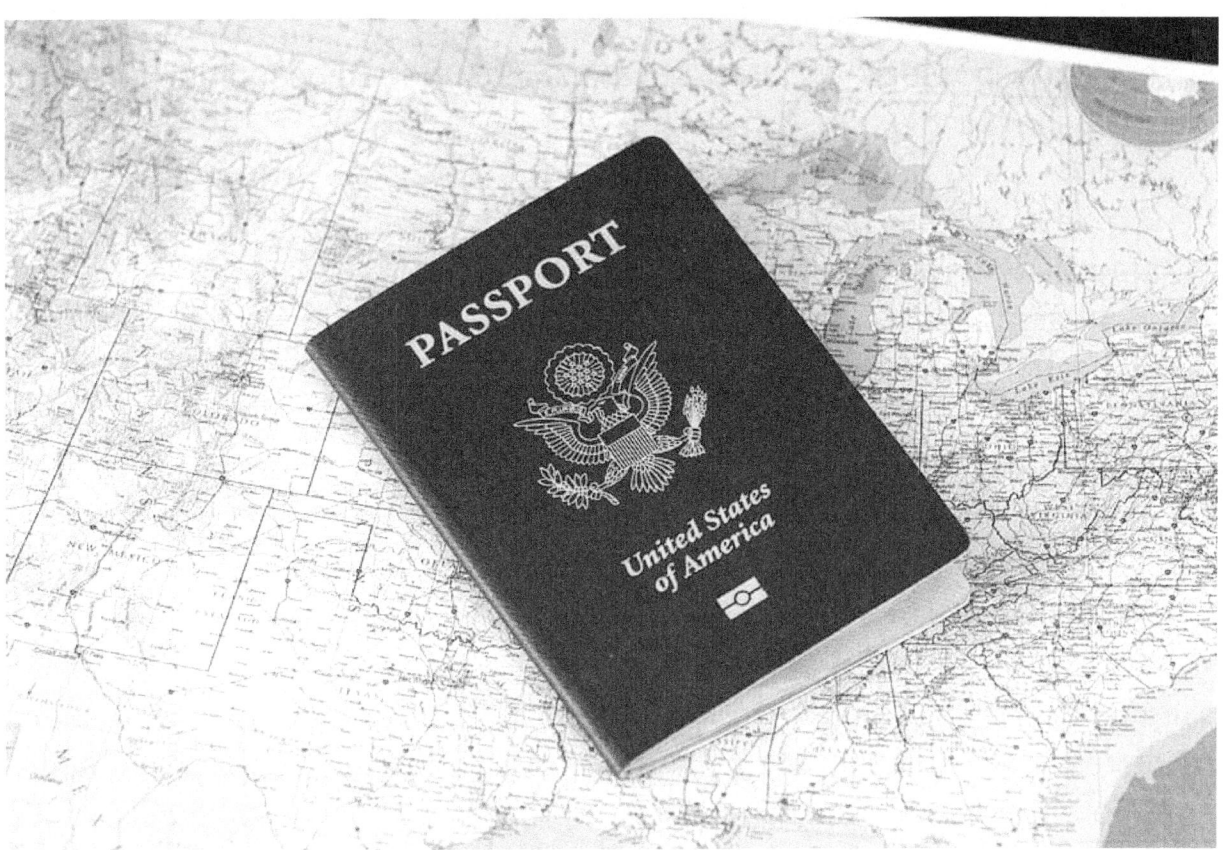

In the realm of air travel, the U.S. government has been toying with updated identification requirements, causing confusion among travelers. The REAL ID Act, which was set to become law on Oct. 1, 2020, has faced numerous changes and delays. The Department of Homeland Security (DHS) now states that all U.S. travelers must meet the REAL ID requirements to board domestic flights by May 7, 2025 (previously May 3, 2023). This begs the question: What does this mean for travelers, and how can you prepare if your ID isn't compliant? In this chapter, we'll clarify these concerns and discuss the use of passports for domestic travel.

Do you need a passport for domestic flights within the U.S. in 2023?
According to the U.S. Transportation Security Administration (TSA), all adult passengers (18 and above) must present valid identification at the airport for travel. This identification should include your picture, name, and

20

state of residence. A passport is not necessarily required for domestic travel within the U.S. in 2023.

If you don't possess a passport, there are other acceptable forms of identification, such as:

- U.S. passport card
- State-issued driver's license
- DHS trusted traveler card
- State-issued Enhanced Driver's License
- U.S. Merchant Mariner Credential
- Border crossing card
- Permanent resident card
- U.S. Department of Defense (DoD) ID
- Tribal-issued photo ID

Surprisingly, even if you have no form of ID due to forgetfulness, loss, or other reasons, you can still fly within the United States. However, you'll need to undergo an identity verification process mandated by the TSA. It's important to note that you will face additional screening, which may be more extensive and time-consuming. Children under 18 years old are not required to provide identification for domestic travel.

What types of ID are necessary for travel within the U.S.?
While you can currently travel within the U.S. using the alternate IDs mentioned above, the situation may change once the REAL ID requirements come into effect in May 2025. At that point, a state-issued ID or driver's license will still be acceptable for boarding flights, but it must bear the REAL ID indication—a star located in the upper left- or right-hand corner. The Department of Homeland Security confirms that all 50 states now issue compliant cards, with most states having achieved compliance within the last four years. If your current ID predates your state's compliance, you can obtain a REAL ID-compliant version upon renewal.

In the absence of a REAL ID, you can use a valid passport, a U.S. military ID, or a federal government PIV card for domestic travel. However, if you choose to use your passport, ensure that it remains valid until May 7, 2025. Passport renewals typically take eight to 11 weeks for routine service or five to seven weeks for expedited service. It's important to plan accordingly, although the Department of State cannot guarantee processing times. Without a passport, a REAL ID-compliant card, or any other accepted form of identification, you will be denied entry through TSA checkpoints, effectively preventing you from flying within the U.S.

Do you need a REAL ID to fly within the U.S.?
Starting on May 7, 2025, all U.S. travelers will require a REAL ID to fly domestically if they do not possess a passport. This ID will also be necessary for accessing federal facilities, including national monuments, federal buildings, and military installations.

This requirement applies to all 50 U.S. states and territories, such as Guam, the U.S. Virgin Islands, the District of Columbia, and Puerto Rico. Although you can still use your passport for domestic flights, this may pose a challenge for the almost 60% of U.S. citizens who lack a passport.

To obtain a REAL ID, visit your local Department of Motor Vehicles office, AAA, or regional state offices. Some states allow pre-application documentation online, so be sure to check the minimum requirements beforehand.

What ID do you need for domestic travel within the U.S.?
As a resident, you'll need a valid passport, driver's license, state ID, or military ID for travel within the U.S. Before your trip, verify the validity of your identification documents. Additionally, familiarize yourself with the laws of the state you're flying to in order to avoid delays and frustrations.

U.S. citizens can also use state-issued enhanced driver's licenses (EDLs) for domestic flights. EDLs are available in select states such as New York,

Washington, Minnesota, Vermont, and Michigan. These licenses are typically issued to residents of states near U.S. borders in compliance with the Western Hemisphere Travel Initiative.

Foreign nationals traveling within the U.S. must present their passports. It is crucial to keep your passport safe during your travels. For foreign nationals, flying within the U.S. without a passport can be quite stressful.

On the other hand, permanent residents (green card holders) need their regular photo ID and green card for domestic travel. The green card can also serve as a driver's license or other form of identification. A passport is not required for domestic travel.

Where can you fly without a passport?
As of March 2023, no states require U.S. citizens to present passports for domestic flights. Airlines and the TSA should not request a valid passport as a mandatory document. However, you can carry your passport as additional photo identification in case other forms of ID are lost.

In summary, you can fly to all 50 U.S. states and territories without a passport. Just make sure to carry your driver's license or state-issued ID. To avoid complications in the future, ensure that your driver's license and other forms of ID comply with the REAL ID standards by May 2025.

For international travel, a passport—ideally stored in a protective holder—is essential. Be cautious not to forget it at home, especially if your travel plans are subject to change.

Chapter 6: The Climate of Arizona

Arizona's climate varies across its different regions, with approximately half of the state being semiarid, one-third arid, and the remainder having a humid climate. The Basin and Range region, known for its arid and semiarid subtropical climate, attracts winter visitors and new residents. In Phoenix, for example, January days are characterized by over four-fifths of possible sunshine and a mean maximum temperature of 65 °F (18 °C). Light frosts occasionally occur in the Basin and Range region during winter, and some precipitation breaks the dryness of spring and fall. In July, daily maximum temperatures in Phoenix average 106 °F (41 °C), with nighttime temperatures dropping to an average of 81 °F (27 °C).

During July, moisture-laden air from the Gulf of California and the eastern Pacific Ocean brings irregular but sometimes heavy thundershowers, known locally as the "summer monsoon." Phoenix and Tucson typically receive about 1 inch (25 mm) of precipitation in July and around 3 inches (75 mm) throughout the summer. Winter rains primarily come from the Pacific.

The Colorado Plateau experiences cool to cold winters and a semiarid climate. The region's average high and low temperatures in January can vary significantly due to its mile-high elevations and exposure to polar air masses. For instance, Winslow can have a mean high temperature of 46 °F (8 °C) and a mean low of 19 °F (−7 °C). Flagstaff, located at higher elevations, is generally about 30 °F (17 °C) cooler than Phoenix year-round. Annual precipitation ranges from 10 to 15 inches (250 to 375 mm) in most parts of the region, with the Mogollon Rim and White Mountains receiving the highest average of 25 inches (625 mm).

The Transition Zone, characterized by diverse relief, exhibits varied climatic conditions over small areas. This zone includes much of Arizona's humid areas and the southern edge of the Colorado Plateau. Shaded riparian corridors and perennial streams contribute to atmospheric moisture, resulting in temperatures several degrees cooler than nearby deserts.

Arizona's vegetation reflects its diverse relief and climate. Forests cover about one-tenth of the state, while woodland and grassland each occupy one-fourth of the land. The remaining portion consists of desert shrub. Elevations above 6,000 to 7,000 feet (1,800 to 2,100 meters) are home to forests of ponderosa pine, with higher areas hosting Douglas and other firs, spruces, and aspen. Piñon pine and juniper dominate the northern half of the state between 4,500 and 7,500 feet (1,375 and 2,300 meters), while evergreen oak and chaparral grow between 4,000 and 6,000 feet (1,400 and 1,800 meters) in the central mountains. Plains grasses cover about one-third of the Colorado Plateau, while Sonoran or desert grass carpets higher elevations in the basins. Mesquite trees have encroached upon former grasslands in the south. Cacti thrive throughout the state, with the greatest diversity found below 2,000 feet (600 meters). The Tucson-Phoenix area's foothills are home to giant saguaro cacti characteristic of the Sonoran Desert, while the northwest Basin and Range region boasts dramatic stands of Joshua trees. Shrubs dominate lower portions of all areas, with big sagebrush and saltbush in the Colorado Plateau and creosote bush in the Basin and Range.

Arizona's animal life is incredibly diverse, representing ecological communities from the Rocky Mountains, Great Plains, and Mexico. Larger mammals include black bears, deer, desert bighorns, antelope, and elk. The coatimundi, a raccoonlike mammal, has expanded northward into Arizona, while the javelina, or peccary, is a popular game animal in the south. Bobcats and mountain lions are notable cat species in Arizona, while coyotes, skunks, and porcupines are abundant. The state is also home to various species of rabbits, jackrabbits, and foxes. The southern border area, located along a major bird migration route, attracts numerous birdwatchers. Game birds such as turkeys, quails, doves, and waterfowl are present, and native fish species include the Arizona trout and Colorado squawfish. Venomous animals such as rattlesnakes, scorpions, and Gila monsters are found in the state.

Arizona's population has a rich cultural diversity, with indigenous peoples playing a significant role. However, urban areas in the state have been heavily influenced by various cultural elements from cities like Chicago, New York City, Washington, D.C., San Francisco, and Los Angeles.

Until the late 19th century, most of central and northern Arizona remained sparsely populated, except for small and scattered groups of indigenous peoples. Spanish presence in the state was limited due to the constant threat posed by hostile Apache bands, with their occupation primarily centered in the Santa Cruz valley south of Tucson.

At the time of Arizona's acquisition by the United States in 1848 as part of New Mexico, the number of Hispanic residents was fewer than 1,000. However, since the 20th century, the Hispanic population has significantly increased, with many Mexicans and their descendants arriving in Arizona since 1900. Relations between Mexican Americans and Anglos (English-speaking whites) have had some strains but have generally been cordial, distinguishing Arizona from other border states. Mexican Americans in Arizona, while preserving elements of Mexican culture, are deeply integrated into the state's business, political, and social life, often intermarrying with Anglos. Native American culture is also prominent in Arizona, with Native Americans comprising less than one-tenth of the state's population. They are organized into 15 tribes residing on 17 reservations, ranging in size from the Tonto Apache reserve, covering 85 acres (34 hectares), to the Navajo reservation spanning 23,400 square miles (60,600 square kilometers), with nearly three-fifths of it located in Arizona. The Navajo tribe, with about 100,000 members in Arizona, actively directs the development of its land and people, assuming responsibility for various aspects of Navajo social and economic life. Other well-known tribes include the Apache and Hopi, while the Tohono O'odham and Akimel O'odham (Pima) peoples have received significant attention in anthropological and historical studies. The Havasupai, Hualapai, Yaqui, and Yavapai are among the lesser-known tribes in the state.

Arizona has a relatively small African American population compared to its total population. Many cities and towns in Arizona have predominantly African American neighborhoods, reflecting de facto housing segregation. The state voluntarily desegregated its schools in the early 1940s. While the Asian and Pacific Islander populations are growing, they still constitute the smallest minority groups in the state.

Settlement patterns in Arizona are primarily concentrated in urban areas, contrary to the romanticized image of picturesque ghost towns, mining camps, isolated ranches, Native American reservations, and idyllic cotton and citrus farms. The majority of the state's population resides in Maricopa County, which includes Phoenix. Six out of the 15 counties collectively house four-fifths of the state's population. The number of people living on farms and ranches is relatively small, and towns and cities generally have low population densities.

Southern Arizona preserves the charm of adobe buildings in its older inhabited areas, while cities like Flagstaff and Prescott in northern Arizona, settled by New Englanders in the 1860s and '70s, feature Victorian-style houses that reflect the preferences and traditions of their early residents.

Phoenix serves as the primary trade center of the state, benefitting from its central location, diverse agricultural economy, and attractive amenities for vacationers and retirees. It has rapidly grown to become one of the largest urban areas in the Southwest. Tucson, although older and smaller than Phoenix, acts as a gateway to Mexico and maintains strong commercial and medical connections with Sonora and other northern Mexican states. Since 1970, Tucson's population growth rate has been comparable to that of Phoenix.

In the early 21st century, Arizona experienced significant population growth at a rate nearly three times the national average. Just over a quarter of the population was under 18 years old. The state attracted new residents, including "snowbirds" who spend winters in the warm desert and return to their primary residences during hot weather. "White flight" from California and out-migration from declining industrial regions in the Midwest and Eastern United States brought working-age individuals to the state. The metropolitan areas, with their maturing economies and high-paying job opportunities, also drew newcomers. Additionally, an unknown number of individuals immigrated illegally, mostly from Mexico and Central America, contributing to the labor force in low-paid service and agricultural sectors. The overall population was projected to reach 10 million by 2027.

Chapter 7: When to Visit Arizona

Arizona offers year-round opportunities for visitors, with different regions experiencing peak seasons at different times. The desert cities like Phoenix and Tucson are most popular from October to mid-May, with the highest hotel rates occurring from January to April. On the other hand, the summer season sees increased activity at the Grand Canyon.

The best times to visit overall are spring and autumn. During these seasons, temperatures are pleasant in the mountains and warm in the desert without extreme heat or cold. However, it's worth noting that late spring and early autumn, specifically May and September, offer additional advantages. These months often have lower rates at desert resorts, taking advantage of the remaining low summer rates, and providing a chance to visit the Grand Canyon with fewer crowds. In spring, you might even witness breathtaking wildflower displays, starting in March and lasting until May, when saguaro cacti bloom with waxy white flowers.

Keep in mind that Sedona experiences colder temperatures in winter, and there's a possibility of snowfall. If you prefer sunny and poolside relaxation, it's advisable to plan your Sedona vacation for a different time of year.

Weather-wise, it's important to know that the desert can be cold as well as hot. While winter is a popular season for tourists in Phoenix and Tucson, nights can be freezing, and some days may not be suitable for outdoor activities. However, overall, winters in Arizona are enjoyable, although higher-elevation areas may have traditional winter weather. It's not uncommon to see snow in the mountains as late as Memorial Day.

In winter, many visitors flock to the deserts, where temperatures average in the high 60s (low 20s Celsius) during the day. During the summer, when desert temperatures soar above 110°F (43°C), the mountains in eastern and northern Arizona provide a pleasant escape with daytime averages in the low 80s (high 20s Celsius). Yuma is known for having the highest winter temperatures in the desert, while Prescott and Sierra Vista, situated at elevations of 4,000 to 6,000 feet, enjoy a temperate climate.

If you find yourself in the desert during July or August, be prepared for sudden thunderstorms and dust storms. These storms can lead to flash floods, temporarily rendering many roads impassable. Pay attention to signs warning about flooded areas and take them seriously.

Avoid venturing into narrow slot canyons, such as Antelope Canyon or the West Fork of Oak Creek Canyon, during potential stormy weather. Even rain falling miles away can trigger flash floods in these narrow canyons without warning. It's crucial to prioritize safety and avoid situations that could put you at risk.

On legal national holidays, certain establishments like banks, government offices, post offices, and many stores, restaurants, and museums may be closed. These holidays include New Year's Day, Martin Luther King, Jr. Day, Presidents' Day, Memorial Day, Independence Day, Labor Day,

Columbus Day, Veterans' Day/Armistice Day, Thanksgiving Day, and Christmas Day. In presidential-election years, the Tuesday after the first Monday in November is Election Day, which is a federal government holiday.

The best times to visit Arizona, from summer sun to winter snow
Arizona, bold, big, and beautiful, offers a variety of experiences throughout the year. Bordered by New Mexico, Utah, Nevada, California, and Mexico, the state enjoys more than 300 days of sunshine and distinct seasons. Whether you seek the summer heat, spring and fall trekking, or winter snow, Arizona has something for everyone.

With its sprawling deserts and majestic mountains, Arizona provides diverse weather conditions year-round, ensuring there's always something to do. However, it's important to note that hotel rates fluctuate during specific times. Spring and fall offer the mildest weather, attracting crowds from all over the state. Although summers can be scorching in the south, low humidity and monsoon rain showers from June to September help alleviate the heat.

Renowned as the gateway to the Grand Canyon, Arizona offers numerous high-elevation hiking trails and mountain wineries in cooler climates. Phoenix, a top winter destination, entices sun-seekers, while Arizona Snowbowl near Flagstaff and other mountain resorts provide excellent skiing opportunities.

To help plan your visit, here are the best times to experience Arizona's wonders:

- October to May: This period is ideal for exploring the Grand Canyon. While temperatures in Tucson and Phoenix can climb above 100°F, higher-altitude areas like Flagstaff and the North Rim of the Grand Canyon National Park remain below 70°F. Spring showcases delicate desert flowers, while fall offers optimal hiking weather. However, these months are also the busiest, resulting in higher hotel prices.

- June to November: This is a great time for desert exploration. Winter temperatures in the northern regions can drop as low as 42°F, dusting higher-elevation cities like Sedona and Flagstaff with snow, signaling the start of the ski season. The Sonoran, Mojave, and Chihuahuan deserts dominate the rest of Arizona. Southern areas experience temperatures ranging from the high 60s to the high 80s. Phoenix, Tucson, and Tombstone serve as excellent bases for exploring these unique arid ecosystems. Start your activities early to avoid the midday heat and increase wildlife spotting opportunities.

- January: Prime skiing weather attracts visitors from colder regions who seek bright sunshine, blue skies, and skiing in Flagstaff and Mount Lemmon near Tucson. It's also an ideal time to experience the annual hot-air balloon festival at Lake Havasu, where balloons drift over London Bridge.
Key events: Sedona Winterfest, Rock 'n' Roll Arizona, Tucson Gem, Fossil & Mineral Showcase, Havasu Balloon Festival

- February: Southern Arizona enjoys pleasant weather in February, luring runners to the Run Sedona Marathon and golf enthusiasts to the fairways at the Phoenix Open. Hotel prices rise as you travel further south, so consider choosing a base outside Phoenix for more affordable options.
Key events: Sedona International Film Festival, Run Sedona Marathon, Waste Management Phoenix Open

- March: Spring in Arizona is perfect for sports, whether actively participating or enjoying as a spectator. Major League Baseball's spring training season in Phoenix is in full swing, and Sedona offers 400 miles of multi-use trails and hosts an annual mountain biking festival.
Key events: Sedona Mountain Bike Festival, Tucson Festival of Books, Cactus League Spring Training

- April: Warm spring temperatures bring the culture scene to life with various events, including music and film festivals, agave appreciation in Tucson, and open artisan studios in Sedona.
Key events: Piano on the Rocks International Festival, Tucson Folk Festival, Agave Heritage Festival, Arizona International Film Festival

- May: As temperatures rise, the desert blooms with cactus flowers, and the wildflower season peaks in May in different areas. Saguaro National Park showcases iconic cacti adorned with white flowers that later produce deep-red fruit. It's also a great time to attend birding events and eco-conscious films for nature enthusiasts.
Key events: Illuminate Film Festival, Southwest Wings Spring Fling, Cinco de Mayo

- June: Before the summer heat sets in, June offers the last opportunity for winter exploration. Hit Arizona's historic highways for road trips to artsy towns and desert sanctuaries. Don't forget to participate in Sedona's annual PhotoFest to capture the state's stunning landscapes.
Key events: Sedona PhotoFest, Made in the Shade, Flagstaff Rodeo, White Mountains Balloon Festival

- July: Arizonans seek cooler weather in July, planning getaways near water bodies for activities like fishing and waterskiing. Weekends are particularly busy with families and day-trippers. Although hotel rates are high, it's worth heading north to immerse yourself in the state's cultural heritage. Flagstaff celebrates Indigenous heritage, while Williams hosts an annual Celtic festival complete with Scottish-style games and bagpiping. Average summer temperatures in Flagstaff hover around 70°F.
Key events: Heritage Festival and Native Art Market, Arizona Highland Games, Sedona Hummingbird Festival

- August: August brings hot temperatures across Arizona, but the desert tends to cool down at night, with minimal humidity. Enjoy moonlit night

hikes, explore museums and art galleries, or unwind in one of Arizona's spas. Alternatively, head to the hills and pine forests for a 10 to 20-degree cooler climate.
Key events: Sedona Photography Symposium, Southeast Arizona Birding Festival

- September: Arizona's thriving wine scene makes September perfect for wine tasting. The Verde Valley, Sonoita, and Willcox offer great tasting rooms. Don't miss out on local wine and food festivals or exploring corn mazes. Keep in mind that accommodations and restaurants can be busy, so book well in advance.
Key events: Arizona Restaurant Week, Harvest Wineopolgy, Sedona Winefest, Red Rocks Music Festival

- October: As Arizona's busy season eases off, October presents an opportunity to find more competitive rates on accommodations. Enjoy slightly cooler days perfect for outdoor festivals celebrating the state's flourishing arts and crafts scene. Craft beer culture takes center stage during Oktoberfest events held throughout the state.
Key events: Sedona Plein Air Festival, Red Rocks Oktoberfest, Sedona Arts Festival, Pride in the Desert

- November: November brings welcome relief from the heat, with slightly cooler temperatures and fewer tourists, at least for a little while. Festivals like the Fountain Festival of Fine Arts & Crafts and Phoenix Pride offer vibrant experiences.
Key events: Phoenix Pride, Fountain Festival of Fine Arts & Crafts, Uncorked Arizona Wine Festival

- December: Arizona embraces the holiday spirit in December, with unique celebrations, even in the desert. Less touristy places may offer moderate rates, and Sedona is relatively quiet during this time. Keep in mind that weekends and winter holidays can drive up costs due to visitors seeking warmer climates in the south and skiing in the north.

Key events: Tlaquepaque Festival of Lights, Arizona Bowl, Holidays at the Heard

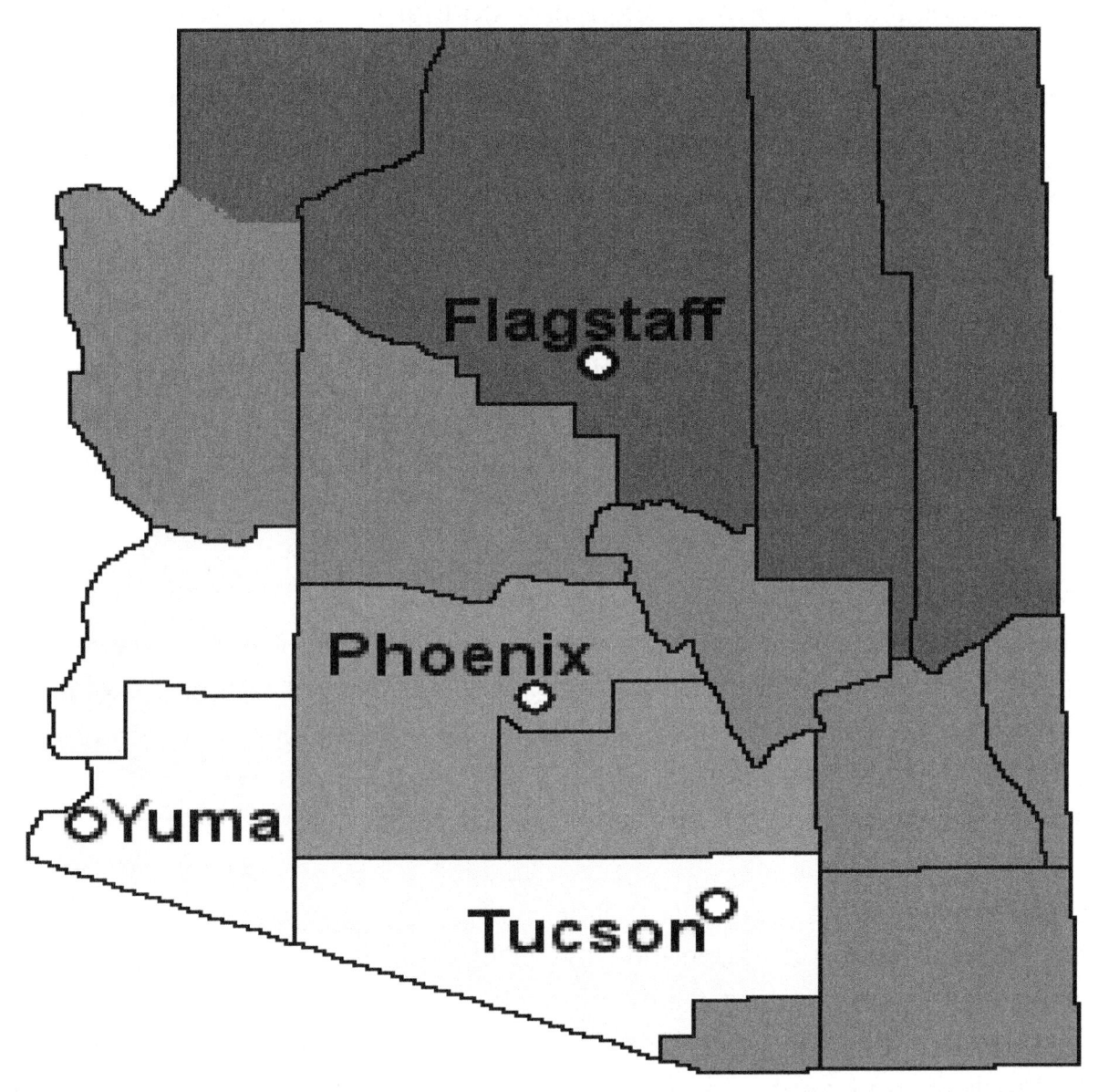

Chapter 8: Must-Visit Destinations in Arizona

Arizona boasts an array of breathtaking destinations that showcase its natural beauty. From the vibrant saguaros in the south to the striking red rock formations up north, there's something for everyone. As a Tucson native, I'm here to help you plan your trip to The Grand Canyon State with my extensive knowledge of the area. Let's dive into the 27 best places to visit in Arizona!

Grand Canyon National Park

No photo can capture the awe-inspiring beauty of the Grand Canyon. It's a must-visit location for anyone exploring northern Arizona. The south rim offers a desert landscape, while the north rim boasts dense forests and wildlife. For an unforgettable adventure, hike from the south rim to the north rim, including a visit to Havasu Falls along the way. Be sure to check out guided tours for more exciting experiences!

Sedona

Known for its magical ambiance and red rock formations, Sedona is a top destination in Arizona. Western-style resorts, vortexes with healing energy, crystal stores, and unique gift shops await you. Explore some of the best hiking trails in the state, including a semi-secret trail leading to "the birthing cave" for incredible views.

Bisbee

A historic copper mining town near Tucson, Bisbee offers a wealth of personality and excitement. Spend a night at the Copper Queen Hotel for a potentially spooky experience, take a thrilling mine tour, and enjoy live music at The Bisbee Social Club. Don't forget to browse the town's numerous antique and thrift stores for unique finds.

Tombstone

Step back in time and experience the Wild West in Tombstone, Arizona's most famous outlaw town. Stroll along the main drag, visit saloons with bullet holes in the ceilings, and explore the Boothill Graveyard for a glimpse into the lives and deaths of Tombstone's residents during the Wild West era.

Flagstaff

Flagstaff, home to Northern Arizona University, offers a charming college town experience. Discover quirky shops, excellent breweries, homestyle restaurants, and abundant outdoor activities. Visit Dark Sky Brewing for a cozy atmosphere or join a stargazing experience at Lowell Observatory. Don't miss the opportunity to go skiing or snowboarding at Arizona

Snowbowl Ski Resort, and explore nearby attractions like The Grand Canyon, Sedona, and Monument Valley.

Saguaro National Park
The Sonoran Desert's defining plant, the saguaro cactus, dominates the landscape at Saguaro National Park. Divided into East and West sections, both areas offer stunning views of thousands of saguaros against majestic mountains. Explore hiking trails such as Wasson Peak and the Yetman Trail, and visit the Arizona Sonora Desert Museum, Old Tucson, and the Arizona Wildlife Museum.

Monument Valley
Located along the Arizona-Utah border, Monument Valley showcases mesmerizing sandstone buttes featured in famous Western movies. Take a scenic drive along the Tribal Park Loop, visit the Monument Valley Visitor Center, and consider a guided tour or horseback ride to fully immerse yourself in this iconic landscape.

Tucson
Tucson, a laidback city surrounded by five mountain ranges in a desert landscape, offers something for everyone. Hiking enthusiasts can explore the endless trails, including those leading to Seven Falls and Romero Pools in the Santa Catalina Mountains or enjoy rock climbing along the Mount Lemmon Scenic Byway. Fourth Avenue and downtown Tucson are vibrant areas where you can immerse yourself in Native American and Hispanic culture through funky shops, breweries, mouthwatering restaurants, museums, and historic sites. Don't miss the picturesque University of Arizona campus, surrounded by bars and boutiques.

Sonoita
Sonoita, a wine lover's paradise, is a scenic getaway just south of Tucson. With its rolling hills, cooler temperatures, and vineyards, it's the perfect destination for couples, friends, or solo travelers. When visiting Sonoita's vineyards, be sure to plan ahead for transportation, such as booking a

designated driver or staying at a nearby bed and breakfast. Consider indulging in a full day of vineyard tours with an affordable limo service for a memorable experience.

Phoenix

As the capital city, Phoenix offers endless attractions to keep visitors busy. From exploring the Desert Botanical Gardens and Phoenix Zoo to enjoying water activities on Tempe Town Lake, there's something for everyone. The city is easily accessible through Sky Harbor International Airport and has a decent public transportation system in place. If you have enough time, consider exploring popular spots in Phoenix over several days. Its central location also makes it convenient for day trips to other Arizona attractions when renting a car.

Scottsdale

Known as the "Beverly Hills of Arizona," Scottsdale is a glamorous destination for luxury resort stays and high-end shopping. The perfectly manicured streets with palm trees, brick sidewalks, and sparkling window displays create a sophisticated atmosphere. Treat yourself to a relaxing spa day at acclaimed resorts or explore Old Town Scottsdale for shopping during the day and vibrant clubbing at night. Although it may be pricier than other destinations, Scottsdale offers a glamorous vacation experience.

Nogales

Located less than an hour south of Tucson, Nogales provides a vibrant border town experience with authentic Mexican culture. Whether enjoying Mexican cuisine, shopping for colorful pottery, or simply immersing yourself in the laidback atmosphere, Nogales offers a taste of Mexico without crossing the border. If you have a passport, consider walking across the border into Nogales, Sonora, to explore its distinct ambiance. Don't miss the opportunity to dine at La Roca, a favorite mountainside restaurant.

Pinetop

Surrounded by a dense pine forest, Pinetop is a charming mountain town perfect for a woodland getaway. Enjoy the crisp mountain air, and if you're a fan of winter sports, indulge in skiing at Sunrise Ski Valley, just 30 minutes away. For a more secluded experience, visit the nearby town of Greer, situated in a small valley with picturesque scenery. Pinetop's proximity to Petrified Forest National Park, just over an hour away, provides an additional attraction for nature enthusiasts.

Page
Page is a hidden gem surrounded by astonishing sandstone formations and the vast Lake Powell. Although it requires some driving to reach this northern destination, it's well worth the effort. Enjoy camping, boat rentals, or kayaking along the banks of Lake Powell. Witness the iconic Horseshoe Bend, a magnificent rock formation shaped by the Colorado River. Another must-visit attraction is Antelope Canyon, where winding sandstone slot canyons create an otherworldly landscape. Vermilion Cliffs National Monument, located less than an hour away, offers more stunning landscapes to explore.

Prescott
Known for its whiskey scene, Prescott is a historic town with well-preserved architecture from the pioneer era. Whiskey Row is famous for its lively music scene and bars. Explore Watson Lake, a popular destination for birding, hiking, biking, and camping, offering breathtaking views of massive boulders and lush greenery. Prescott is an ideal place for those seeking a combination of rich history and natural beauty.

Jerome
Explore Jerome, the captivating ghost town with a fascinating history. Once a thriving copper mining town, Jerome's downfall and eerie tales make it a must-visit for ghost town enthusiasts. Take a ghost tour to uncover the town's spooky stories and visit the Mine Museum and Jerome State Historic Park for a glimpse into its past. Wander through the downtown area, which is adorned with unique art galleries, gift shops, and occasional live music.

Saguaro Lake

Escape to the picturesque oasis of Saguaro Lake, surrounded by towering canyon walls and blooming saguaro cacti. Located in the Tonto National Forest near Mesa, this desert lake offers a refreshing retreat. Rent kayaks, speedboats, paddleboards, or other water gear from Precision Marina for a fun-filled day on the lake. Saguaro Lake is the perfect destination for a leisurely date or a family outing.

Lake Pleasant

Experience the vastness of Lake Pleasant, offering endless opportunities for water sports. Situated just 40 minutes north of central Phoenix, this popular attraction is easily accessible. Enjoy activities such as paddleboarding, rowing, or embark on an all-inclusive cruise. Scorpion Bay features Paqua Park, an exhilarating obstacle course suitable for all ages. While the kids have a blast at Paqua Park, relax on a peaceful boat nearby.

Lake Havasu City

Discover the beach paradise of Lake Havasu, known as the best beach destination in the desert. With its scenic beauty and numerous attractions, Lake Havasu is a favorite among visitors. The city revolves around the lake, offering various water activities and iconic sights such as the London Bridge. Engage in wakeboarding, jet skiing, or rent a houseboat for a complete Havasu vacation. Just avoid visiting during spring break for a more peaceful experience.

Montezuma Castle National Monument

Immerse yourself in the resilient Native American history at Montezuma Castle National Monument. These well-preserved dwellings, built by the Sinagua people around 1,000 years ago, offer a fascinating glimpse into the past. Located in Camp Verde, the dwellings built into the mountainside create a unique and captivating experience. This national monument is a must-visit for history buffs and those interested in American Indian culture.

Organ Pipe Cactus National Monument
Experience the stunning environment of Organ Pipe Cactus National Monument, home to unique cactus plants. The only place in the United States where these massive cacti grow wild, this UNESCO biosphere reserve is located just north of the Mexican border. Take a moment to visit the visitor center before exploring the area or continuing your journey south to Puerto Peñasco.

Chiricahua National Monument
Embark on a memorable hiking and camping adventure in the captivating Chiricahua National Monument. This extraordinary national monument showcases a vast mountain range eroded into impressive hoodoos, resembling natural pillars. With 17 miles of scenic hiking trails, Chiricahua offers awe-inspiring views and the chance to encounter fascinating wildlife. Whether in Arizona or elsewhere, this unique destination is a hiker's dream.

Payson
Escape the heat and immerse yourself in the cool mountain town of Payson. The drive from Phoenix to Payson is a scenic route through the Four Peaks Wilderness, featuring wildflowers and desert wildlife. Enjoy a relaxing picnic or take a refreshing dip at Water Wheel Falls, a beautiful spot just north of Payson. Petrified Forest National Park is also within reach, making Payson an ideal destination for outdoor lovers.

Winslow
Take a step back in time and explore Winslow, a small Arizona town along historic Route 66. With its connection to the classic Eagles song "Take It Easy," Winslow has become a popular tourist destination. Spend a few hours exploring the local businesses, including the historic trading post, to learn about the town's past. Don't forget to visit the Petrified Forest National Park, located just under an hour away.

Oatman

Experience the charm of Oatman, an authentic western town located along Route 66. Once a mining camp, Oatman is now home to friendly burros that roam freely through the streets. Witness the thrilling Oatman Ghost Rider Gunfights, daily reenactments of old western drama. Explore the historic downtown area, including the museum at the Oatman Hotel, to learn about the town's exciting mining history in the Black Mountains.

Eloy

Discover the ultimate skydiving destination in Eloy, which proudly houses the world's largest skydiving facility. While there may not be many other attractions in this small Arizona city, adventurers seeking a challenge can venture to Picacho Peak State Park, located less than an hour away, for a difficult hike.

If you've ever dreamt of leaping from a plane over the stunning Sonoran Desert, Eloy is the place to make it a reality. Skydive Arizona welcomes over 100,000 jumpers annually and boasts some of the most highly-trained instructors in the country. Whether you're a beginner or an experienced diver, join other skydiving enthusiasts and perhaps even set a new world record.

Wilcox

Experience a delightful fall-weather wonderland in Wilcox, renowned for its apple orchards and pumpkin patches. As autumn arrives, both visitors and locals eagerly flock to Wilcox from Tucson to indulge in picking fresh fruit from the famous orchards. Apple Annies, a cherished family-run operation with three locations in the basin, offers a fantastic opportunity for family-friendly fun.

Downtown Wilcox captivates with its historic charm, featuring antique shops, local businesses, museums, and wineries showcasing the region's vineyards. You can easily spend a fulfilling day in this serene Arizona town, immersing yourself in its tranquil atmosphere.

Pro Tip: Ensure you check the orchard's opening hours to plan your visit during the peak season.

Chapter 9: Top 10 Places To Visit In Arizona For An Action-Packed Vacay

Arizona prides itself on being a paradise filled with architectural marvels, natural wonders, and an abundance of vibrancy and elegance. With a diverse range of captivating geological formations and canyons, Arizona's attractions are truly worth exploring. The state is renowned for its world-famous and immensely majestic sights, including the Grand Canyon, Havasu Falls, Cathedral Rock, Hoover Dam, and Monument Valley, which enhance the overall beauty of Arizona. Whether you opt for hiking to discover the lush waterfalls of Havasu Falls or indulge in thrilling water sports at Lake Powell and Clarkdale, Arizona offers endless adventures for the adventurous spirit within you. With a plethora of places to visit, it's easy to run short on time. As you plan your trip to Arizona, let's take a tour of some of the best attractions that will undoubtedly make you fall head over heels in love with this beautiful land.

Top 10 Arizona Tourist Attractions
We have carefully selected some of the finest places to visit in Arizona to help you plan your trip to the Grand Canyon State in the best possible way!

1. Grand Canyon

Renowned worldwide for its magnificent beauty, the Grand Canyon offers breathtaking vistas that will surely enchant you. This awe-inspiring landscape, carved by the Colorado River, presents incredible views of magically formed rock formations as you stand on the rim. Wherever you go, you will encounter the fossilized remains of various plants and animals. Interestingly, you can choose to hike down into the Grand Canyon or opt for a helicopter flight to experience a closer look at this marvelous creation of nature.

2. Sedona

Situated amidst captivating red sandstone mountains and buttes, Sedona is unquestionably one of the best places to visit in Arizona. With its beautiful setting, this place astounds travelers from all over the world and is considered an extremely spiritual site famous for its energy vortexes. Explore the numerous shops offering alternative medicines, and indulge in relaxation at one of the many spas to rejuvenate yourself. For adventure enthusiasts, don't miss out on cycling, hiking, or swimming in the serene waters.

3. Phoenix

Nestled amidst the desert and known as "the Valley of the Sun," Phoenix has much to offer. As the economic and cultural heart of the state, it boasts a multitude of entertaining museums and theaters that will captivate art lovers. Abundant shopping options beckon travelers to embark on a delightful shopping spree. Don't forget to explore the best restaurants and bars, where you can indulge in global delicacies. A visit to Phoenix guarantees you'll never have a dull moment.

4. Havasu Falls

Located near the isolated village of Supai, Havasu Falls is a breathtaking waterfall that flows through Havasupai land in the Havasu Canyon. This mesmerizing waterfall features a single cataract plunging about 120 feet into a natural swimming pool. The unique feature of this waterfall is its blue-green water that beautifully complements the backdrop of the red canyon wall. You can choose to reach this stunning place via a helicopter ride, a horseback ride, or a 13 km hike.

5. Antelope Canyon

If you're looking for the best places to visit in Arizona, Antelope Canyon should definitely be on your checklist. The distorted and twisted cracks of Antelope Canyon will make you believe that nature itself is a remarkable designer. As you wander around the sandstone walls, you'll encounter sunbeams gracefully sneaking their way through, adorning the walls with sparkling lights. It's truly a visual treat, and the canyon is aptly nicknamed "The Crack" and "The Corkscrew," each showcasing its unique beauty that impresses visitors.

6. Saguaro National Park

Adding a unique charm to Arizona's tourist attractions, Saguaro National Park spans approximately 91,000 acres of the Sonoran desert in Tucson. You'll be astounded by the renowned saguaro cacti up close, but there's more to admire in this park. Explore various historic sights, prehistoric petroglyphs, and the beautiful wildlife that make your trip to Arizona worthwhile. Within the park's boundaries, you can also enjoy adventurous activities such as hiking, picnicking, and wildlife spotting.

7. Monument Valley

Famous as a backdrop for numerous western movies, including Forrest Gump, Jurassic World: Fallen Kingdom, and Wild America, Monument Valley is an iconic attraction in Arizona. Straddling the border between Utah and Arizona, this site is adorned with spiked rock formations, sand dunes, and stone spires and buttes. Nestled in the heart of the valley is the Monument Valley Navajo Tribal Park, which includes a visitor center. To explore the area like a pro, opt for a guided tour that delves into the history of this remarkable place.

8. Tombstone

Offering a contemporary glimpse of an Old West town, Tombstone is a famous historic site. Staged gunfights in the streets and characters dressed in period costumes bring the glittering days of this petite Arizona town back to life. The property features various hotels, souvenir shops, restaurants, salons, and entertainment hubs, providing visitors with a glimpse of the town's rich history. Historical sites like Boothill Graveyard, Tombstone Courthouse State Historic Park, and O.K. Corral will transport you to another era, making it hard to leave this captivating place.

9. Hoover Dam

Touted as one of the engineering marvels, Hoover Dam is nestled between Nevada and Arizona on the Colorado River. This colossal concrete dam was constructed to control flooding, provide irrigated water, and generate electricity. Visit the visitor center to learn about the dam's construction and take an elevator ride into the canyon wall to witness the power plant. To satisfy your hunger, there's a café offering a wide range of food options.

10. Lake Powell

Situated on the border between Utah and Arizona, Lake Powell is one of the finest man-made reservoirs. It came into existence following the construction of Glen Canyon Dam, which led to the flooding of Glen Canyon. Today, it is considered one of the top destinations in Arizona. If adventure is on your mind, you must visit this destination and take part in various activities such as hiking, jet skiing, fishing, waterskiing, and boating. A visit to Lake Powell promises an action-packed day amidst stunning natural surroundings.

Chapter 10: Exclusive Outdoor Adventures You Can Only Have in Arizona

Arizona offers an array of thrilling experiences that will leave you wanting more. From the legendary Lost Dutchman's Gold Mine to longboarding down Mt. Lemmon and hiking the Grand Canyon Rim-to-Rim, there's something for every adventure seeker. Check out this list to discover your next thrilling mission.

1. Embarking on the Havasu Canyon Trail Hike

Beneath the rim of the Grand Canyon, lies the captivating Havasu Canyon with its five awe-inspiring waterfalls. These waterfalls boast a vibrant blue-green hue that even Crayola couldn't replicate. Whether you choose to hike, ride a horse, or take a helicopter to the falls, the challenging 8-mile journey from Hualapai Hilltop to the water demands effort, but rewards you with breathtaking views. Once inside the canyon, a dirt trail leads you to turquoise swimming holes and towering waterfalls that reach up to 200 feet in height.

For the past 800 years, the Havasupai tribe, also known as the "People of the Blue-Green Waters," has called this place home, caring for the falls and the land around them. When visiting, remember that this destination holds deep significance to the Havasupai people and their cultural identity.

2. Discovering the Enchanting Verde Hot Springs

Verde Hot Springs is a well-kept local secret in Arizona. Once a part of a hotel nestled into a mountain overlooking the Verde River, these springs hold tales of the past. Although the hotel burned down in the '60s, it left behind a legacy and two pools located within the remains of its foundation. The larger pool offers an open-air experience, providing sweeping views of the Verde River and the valley beyond. Meanwhile, the smaller, warmer pool resides inside a small roofless building adorned with psychedelic paintings.

Part of the adventure of reaching Verde Hot Springs is the journey itself. The unmaintained Fossil Creek Road winds through the barren desert mountains, offering a bone-shaking ride that can test your vehicle's suspension. As you drive along Fossil Creek Road after turning off Route 260, take your time to appreciate the waterfalls, swimming holes, and hiking trails located just off the road.

Once you reach the campground, you'll embark on another mile of hiking before crossing the river to reach the springs. If it's your first time, it's best to make the crossing during daylight hours. Follow the river towards the old power plant, and keep an eye out for stacks of rocks left by fellow adventurers, or use your intuition to find a calm spot in the river for crossing. Remember, help is far away if you find yourself with a sprained ankle, so proceed with caution.

3. Mountain Biking in Prescott

Prescott, a northern Arizona town, has become a premier destination for mountain biking enthusiasts. The town boasts an impressive network of 250 miles of trails, catering to riders of all skill levels, from gentle slopes suitable for beginners to challenging and rugged terrains for the most seasoned riders. Prescott's mountain biking scene comes alive during the annual Whiskey Off-Road event held every April, featuring a three-day endurance race, live music, and, of course, whiskey.

What makes Prescott particularly enticing for cyclists is the diversity of its trails. Within a relatively small area, you can find yourself cruising down smooth downhill slopes, tackling demanding cross-country routes, or navigating technical hills. The Willow Dells Slickrock Trails, known for their challenging yet rewarding nature, wind their way through the otherworldly Granite Dells. These unique rock formations rise from the earth, resembling eroded drip castles. During the early mornings and evenings, the tranquil waters of Willow Creek reflect these formations, creating a surreal ambiance.

4. Embarking on a Whitewater Rafting Adventure in the Grand Canyon
While the rim views of the Grand Canyon are remarkable, truly experiencing this natural wonder requires floating through its depths. Over millions of years, the Colorado River has tirelessly carved out the magnificent canyon, offering one of the most epic whitewater routes on the planet.

Grand Canyon rapids predate the modern Class VI rating scale, and this is one of the few places in the world where you can encounter Class 10 whitewater, depending on the water conditions. Rapids like Crystal and Lava Falls, considered some of the most challenging on the Colorado, can achieve this rating. Regardless of the section you choose to raft and the time of your adventure, you'll encounter thrilling rushes that rival the best amusement parks and witness breathtaking views unique to Arizona.

5. Off-Roading Adventure in Sedona's Red Rocks

Imagine a scene where the Greek gods, including Zeus, debate whether to settle on Mount Olympus or among the striking red rocks of Sedona. As the evening descends, these massive formations transform into an intense shade of red, inspiring contemplation and attracting New Age enthusiasts from around the world.

While many beautiful views in Sedona are accessible from the road, a whole new world unfolds when you have an off-road vehicle and a knowledgeable guide. Several companies offer jeep tours that venture into remote locations amidst the red rocks. These tours typically last two to three hours and take you to sweeping desert vistas and the ancient ruins of Native American dwellings.

6. Relaxing and Floating along the Salt River
Floating along the Salt River has become a beloved tradition in the Phoenix area. Don't expect rapids or ancient ruins—instead, picture happy weekenders, sipping on beers, engaging in friendly conversations, and having a fantastic time.

The river winds through the scenic Tonto National Forest, providing an easy escape from the city. Just a half-hour drive from Phoenix, you can leave your vehicle behind, rent tubes, and catch a bus to the drop-off point. As you float through the desert landscape, the duration of your journey can range from two to four hours. Remember to pack plenty of water in your cooler and protect yourself from the intense Arizona sunshine by wearing a cap.

7. Soaring over the Sonoran Desert in a Hot-Air Balloon
How do you overcome the challenges posed by the desert—its thorny plants, venomous creatures, and scorching temperatures—to fully appreciate the awe-inspiring landscape that is home to the only population of jaguars in the United States? You rise above it all—literally.

Hot-air balloon tours operate throughout Arizona, but the opportunity to witness the Sonoran Desert in southern Arizona from the sky is particularly enticing. Start your adventure early in the morning to witness one of the most captivating sunrises imaginable. As the sun ascends, keep your eyes peeled for sightings of Sonoran pronghorns, coyotes, and javelinas down below.

8. Experiencing the Thrill of Skydiving

If soaring in a hot-air balloon wasn't enough, take your aerial adventure to the next level by boarding a plane for a skydiving experience. Thanks to Arizona's warm climate and consistently clear skies, the state has become a hotspot for skydiving enthusiasts. Even experienced skydivers from Europe come here to indulge in desert jumps at various sites located between Tucson and Phoenix. Whether you're a first-timer seeking a tandem jump or a seasoned veteran of the skies, skydiving in Arizona promises the ultimate adrenaline rush.

9. Unwind on a Dude Ranch and Ride off into the Sunset

Staying at a dude ranch in Arizona offers the perfect blend of outdoor adventure suitable for the whole family and the amenities typically found in all-inclusive resorts. Ranches typically offer guided horse tours of the surrounding lands. Depending on the ranch, you may find yourself herding cattle, embarking on desert hikes, or even playing a round of golf on a world-class course. As the sun sets, your belly will be full from delicious meals, and you can revel in the spectacle of a sky

At the end of each day, riding off into the sunset while gazing at the crowded parking lot of stars above, marking a perfect end to a day filled with outdoor adventure.

10. Exploring the Enigmatic Chiricahua National Monument

Nestled in the southeastern corner of Arizona, Chiricahua National Monument is a mesmerizing expanse of volcanic rock spires. The sight of boulders precariously perched atop one another can defy the laws of physics, creating an otherworldly atmosphere.

Encompassing around 12,000 acres, this area holds historical significance as it once served as a refuge for Geronimo, the famed Native American warrior, and his Apache comrades, who strategized and launched attacks against the encroaching U.S. Army. Today, the national monument stands out for its captivating hiking trails and opportunities for birdwatching, offering glimpses of majestic bald eagles and swift prairie falcons. Don't miss the awe-inspiring view from Massai Point, which promises an unrivaled perspective.

Chapter 11: Recreational Activities In Arizona

Arizona offers a wide range of recreational activities that cater to various interests and preferences. From exploring the breathtaking natural landscapes to engaging in thrilling outdoor adventures, there is something for everyone. Here are some of the popular recreational activities in Arizona:

1. Hiking and Nature Walks: With its diverse terrain, Arizona is a hiker's paradise. From the iconic trails of the Grand Canyon to the red rocks of Sedona and the Sonoran Desert's vast wilderness, there are countless trails to explore and enjoy breathtaking views.

2. Rock Climbing: Arizona's rugged cliffs and canyons provide excellent opportunities for rock climbing enthusiasts. Places like Mount Lemmon near Tucson and Oak Creek Canyon in Sedona offer challenging routes for climbers of all skill levels.

3. Water Sports: Arizona may be known for its desert landscapes, but it also boasts several lakes and rivers that are perfect for water activities. Lake Powell, the Colorado River, and the Salt River are popular spots for boating, kayaking, paddleboarding, and jet skiing.

4. Off-Roading: The state's vast network of trails and open desert areas makes off-roading a thrilling adventure. Visitors can rent ATVs, dirt bikes, or Jeeps to explore the rugged backcountry, sand dunes, and desert trails.

5. Wildlife Viewing: Arizona is home to a rich diversity of wildlife. Visitors can go birdwatching, spot elusive desert animals like javelinas and roadrunners, or observe larger mammals such as elk and bighorn sheep in their natural habitats.

6. Golfing: Arizona boasts numerous world-class golf courses, including championship-level layouts designed by renowned architects. The pleasant weather and stunning desert scenery make it an ideal destination for golf enthusiasts.

7. Hot Air Ballooning: Experience the beauty of Arizona from above by taking a hot air balloon ride. Drifting gently over the picturesque landscapes of Sedona, Phoenix, or the Sonoran Desert offers a unique and memorable adventure.

8. Cultural and Historical Sites: Arizona has a rich Native American heritage, and visitors can explore ancient ruins, such as the cliff dwellings at Montezuma Castle National Monument or the UNESCO World Heritage site of Tumacácori National Historical Park.

9. Stargazing: Arizona's clear skies and low light pollution make it a fantastic destination for stargazing. Observatories and astronomy centers offer educational programs and opportunities to view celestial wonders.

10. Spa and Wellness Retreats: The state is home to numerous luxury resorts and wellness retreats where visitors can relax and rejuvenate. Enjoy spa treatments, yoga classes, and meditation sessions while surrounded by tranquil desert landscapes.

11. Fishing: Immerse yourself in a day of fishing in the mountain lakes surrounded by serene Ponderosa pine forests. Whether you prefer casting from the bank, wading in the water, or setting up camp on the ice, this is the ideal spot.

12. Horseback Riding: For those who believe that four feet are better than two, saddle up and enjoy a horseback ride through the stunning White Mountains of Arizona.

13. Hunting: The Apache-Sitgreaves National Forest is home to a variety of animals for which hunting permits are issued.

13. Motorized Trail Riding: The White Mountain region offers over 60 miles of trails, specially groomed for ATV, OHV, and snowmobiling adventures. From Clay Springs to Pinetop-Lakeside, there's plenty of excitement for thrill-seekers.

14. Mountain Biking: If you prefer the thrill of riding on two wheels, the White Mountains Trail System features over 200 miles of non-motorized, multi-use trails. Mountain biking enthusiasts of all skill levels flock to this area to experience the exhilarating single-track trails and the natural beauty of the pine-filled surroundings.

15. Bird Watching: Wherever you are in the White Mountains, you'll have ample opportunities to observe birds in their numnbers. In this region alone, there are more than 400 species waiting to be discovered and admired.

These are just a few examples of the recreational activities available in Arizona. Whether you seek outdoor adventures, cultural exploration, or simply want to unwind in a serene environment, Arizona provides an abundance of options to cater to every interest and create unforgettable experiences.

Chapter 12: Arizona — History and Culture

Arizona exudes a quintessential southwestern culture that sets it apart. What makes this state truly exceptional is the fascinating fusion of Native American, Mexican, frontier, and contemporary influences. From the vibrant streets of Phoenix to ancient cliff dwellings, Arizona showcases a diverse culture that rivals that of any other state in the nation.

Historical Background

European exploration of Arizona began in the 14th and 15th centuries, as Spanish explorers ventured north from Mexico. These expeditions primarily aimed at colonization and spreading Christianity. In 1821, Mexico gained independence from Spain, and the Arizona region became part of New California.

Following the Mexican-American War in 1847, the United States gained control of the territory, which then fell under the jurisdiction of New Mexico. The southern portion of Arizona, acquired through the Gadsden Purchase of 1853, briefly seceded from the territory during the American Civil War. Finally, on February 14, 1912, Arizona achieved statehood, becoming the 48th and final contiguous state to join the Union.

Economic Development

Arizona's economic prosperity traces back to the mining industry in the 17th century. Thousands of fortune-seekers flocked to the state during the gold and silver rushes in the Western United States. In the late 1800s and early 1900s, cotton, copper, and ranching emerged as key drivers of the economy. The legendary "wild west" culture flourished during this frontier era.

While the ranching and copper industries faced challenges during the Great Depression, tourism began to thrive. The arrival of the Santa Fe Railroad at the Colorado River in the early 20th century opened up Arizona's remarkable landscapes to the rest of the country. The Grand Canyon, in particular, became an iconic symbol of the state, and tourism soon became a cornerstone of Arizona's economy.

In the post-war period, Arizona experienced significant population growth and economic stability due to an influx of retirees. The warm climate, the advent of air conditioning, and the development of extensive water infrastructure made Arizona an appealing destination. To delve deeper into Arizona's history, visit the Arizona History Museum in Tucson or explore the pioneering heritage at Flagstaff's Riordan Mansion.

Cultural Diversity

Arizona's culture is a captivating tapestry woven from the influences of neighboring states. While Phoenix serves as the contemporary hub of the state, it is renowned for its striking desert landscapes, natural landmarks, and strong Mexican influences. The cuisine of Arizona reflects a harmonious blend of Western and Mexican flavors, and the presence of Native American craftsmanship is evident throughout the region.

Visitors to major cities like Phoenix, Tucson, and Flagstaff can immerse themselves in Native American heritage through tours of ancient sites. However, the essence of Arizona's travel culture lies in its sunny climate and natural wonders shaped by Mother Nature. Outdoor enthusiasts can revel in exhilarating adventures at Grand Canyon National Park, San Francisco Peaks, and Meteor Crater, which offer year-round excitement for tourists.

Chapter 13: Best Cultural Attractions in Scottsdale and Phoenix Arizona

Arizona is an enchanting state that captivates visitors with its remarkable attractions. Two cities, Scottsdale and Phoenix, epitomize the allure of this region. Located in Maricopa County, eastern Arizona, these cities are a haven for spa enthusiasts and golf lovers. However, it's important to note that while both cities attract tourists year-round, the winter and spring seasons are particularly popular.

1. MIM – Musical Instruments Museum, Phoenix, Arizona

If you've always been fascinated by musical instruments or have a penchant for museums, the MIM (Musical Instruments Museum) in Phoenix is a must-visit. This cultural gem showcases over 15,000 musical instruments, setting a record in its vast collection. Immerse yourself in the exhibits that feature instruments and attire from renowned musicians worldwide. You can even try your hand at playing some instruments in the interactive Experience Gallery. Explore the museum's second floor, where instruments are organized by geographic region, offering an educational and enjoyable experience.

2. Taliesin West
Discover the architectural legacy of Frank Lloyd Wright at Taliesin West, a historic landmark in Scottsdale. This former residence served as Wright's headquarters and provides a glimpse into his vision of an ideal living, working, and learning space. Set against the backdrop of the Arizonian desert, Taliesin West showcases a captivating blend of contemporary and rustic design. Visitors can admire the remarkable architectural features and participate in programs that delve into the world of architecture and Wright's works.

3. Heard Museum
For those intrigued by American Indian history and culture, the Heard Museum in Phoenix is a must-see. This museum is dedicated to advancing and celebrating American Indian art, providing a unique firsthand perspective on their traditions and heritage. If you visit in November, don't miss the annual El Mercado de Las Artes festival, or plan a trip in March to experience the Indian Fair and Market. Immerse yourself in the rich and vibrant experience of American Indian culture.

4. Phoenix Art Museum
Phoenix is a hub of cultural experiences, and the Phoenix Art Museum stands out as a captivating destination. Explore the extensive collection of art spanning different periods, including Victorian, Renaissance, modern, and postmodern works. Walk through the halls and embrace the journey through history and artistic expression. For art enthusiasts and history buffs alike, the Phoenix Art Museum offers a rewarding learning experience.

5. Desert Botanical Garden
The Desert Botanical Garden defies expectations by showcasing the beauty and diversity of desert flora. Despite the arid climate, this botanical garden features an impressive collection of desert plants, trees, flowers,

and shrubs that create vibrant displays of color throughout the year. From cacti to Brittlebush, you'll encounter a wide array of desert plant species, including surprising hues of pink, purple, orange, and blue that harmonize with Arizona's breathtaking sunsets. Don't miss the opportunity to explore the Desert Botanical Garden while hiking in the nearby mountains.

6. Phoenix Symphony Hall

Indulge your love for classical music at Phoenix Symphony Hall, an exquisite concert venue located in Downtown Phoenix. While it serves as a multi-purpose performing arts venue, it is primarily renowned for hosting the Phoenix Symphony Orchestra, the only full-time professional orchestra in Arizona. Immerse yourself in the enchanting melodies of the orchestra or enjoy a romantic evening in this magnificent hall.

7. Cosanti Originals

Discover the artistic world of Paolo Soleri at Cosanti Originals, an art gallery nestled between the Phoenix Mountains Reserve and Scottsdale. This gallery is far from ordinary, showcasing Soleri's unique ideas and vibrant designs. As a student of Frank Lloyd Wright, Soleri's flair is evident throughout the gallery, which is decorated in earthy tones. Take a piece of his exquisite work home by purchasing one of the intricately designed bells, a specialty of Cosanti Originals.

8. Old Town Scottsdale

Immerse yourself in the cultural traditions of Arizona by visiting Old Town Scottsdale. This charming neighborhood features brick buildings adorned in classic styles that pay homage to the past. Take a leisurely stroll through the area and absorb the vibrant atmosphere. Old Town Scottsdale also surprises visitors with its lively nightlife, making it an exciting destination to explore day and night.

9. Scottsdale Museum of the West

Located in Old Town Scottsdale, the Scottsdale Museum of the West offers a comprehensive exploration of the history of the American West. With rotating exhibits that highlight the legacies of figures like Lewis & Clark and showcase bronze artistry, visitors gain valuable insights into this captivating era. The museum also offers self-guided audio tours, allowing you to discover at your own pace.

10. First Friday Art Walk

For art enthusiasts, the First Friday Art Walk is a familiar concept. In Phoenix, Arizona, you can join the First Friday Art Walk and explore numerous galleries showcasing new exhibits. As you stroll through the neighborhood, you'll not only encounter captivating art pieces but also encounter food vendors, jewelers, and local businesses offering unique trinkets and knick-knacks for sale. The First Friday Art Walk is like immersing yourself in a vibrant festival of art and culture.

11. Roosevelt Row

To further attest to Phoenix's artistic charm, visit Roosevelt Row in Downtown Phoenix. This collection of lively streets features historic buildings that proudly exhibit their unique styles. From art galleries to restaurants, Roosevelt Row exudes the charm of Phoenix's rich artistic heritage.

12. Arizona Science Center

For knowledge seekers and science enthusiasts, the Arizona Science Center is an absolute delight. This interactive venue offers a variety of engaging programs and exhibits that cater to both adults and children. Explore the Astronaut Exhibition, gaze at the wonders of the universe in the Dorrance Planetarium, or enjoy a captivating IMAX movie at the onsite theater. The Arizona Science Center is a perfect destination for those eager to learn and indulge their curiosity.

13. Scottsdale Art Walk

The Scottsdale Art Walk is a highly anticipated community art event that draws visitors, buyers, and artists alike. With 28 galleries and two museums participating, the Scottsdale Art Walk offers a diverse and enriching art experience. Stay engaged with the art community by attending the exciting events frequently hosted during the Scottsdale Art Walk. It is truly one of the finest cultural attractions in the area.

Chapter 14: 10 Cultural Hotspots To Visit In Arizona

Arizona is not only known for its stunning natural landscapes but also for its rich cultural heritage. From ancient Native American civilizations to vibrant modern art scenes, the state offers a wide range of cultural hotspots that are worth exploring. Here is a brief introduction to 10 cultural hotspots to visit in Arizona:

Phoenix Art Museum

Since its establishment in 1959, the Phoenix Art Museum has been dedicated to connecting people with great art to enhance their lives. It has grown to become the largest art institution in Arizona, renowned internationally. The museum features temporary exhibitions showcasing the work of both international and American artists, alongside its impressive permanent collection of over 17,000 artworks spanning various genres, including American, Asian, European, Latin American, and modern and contemporary art. The museum also hosts festivals, live performances, independent art films, and educational programs catering to diverse cultural interests.

1625 N. Central Avenue, Phoenix, AZ 85004-1685, +1 602 257-1222

Scottsdale Museum of Contemporary Art
Located in Downtown Scottsdale, the Scottsdale Museum of Contemporary Art (SMoCA) presents exhibitions that not only encompass fine arts but also include works by significant contemporary architects and designers. By juxtaposing various disciplines, SMoCA encourages visitors to explore connections and new perspectives on contemporary innovation. The museum's offerings expanded in 2012 with the addition of the SMoCA Lounge, a community space fostering creativity, imagination, and contemplation. Alongside plastic arts, the lounge hosts literary readings, live music, film screenings, lunchtime lectures, and fundraising events, fostering active engagement beyond mere observation.

7374 E 2nd St, Scottsdale, AZ 85251, +1 480-874-4666

Heard Museum

Founded in 1929 by Dwight B. and Maie Bartlett Heard, the Heard Museum aims to educate the public on the arts, heritage, and traditions of the indigenous people of the American Southwest. The museum's extensive collection of artifacts and art serves as a platform for showcasing the rich cultural history of Native American tribes. Highly regarded internationally, the Heard Museum presents high-quality exhibitions, educational programs, and festivals. By collaborating with American Indian artists and tribal communities, the museum provides an authentic portrayal of native cultures through storytelling and the display of artworks.

2301 N Central Ave, Phoenix, AZ 85004, +1 602-252-8840

Mesa Arts Center

As Arizona's largest multidisciplinary arts venue, the Mesa Arts Center encompasses four performance theaters, five exhibition galleries, and 14 art studios within an impressive architectural complex. The center's exhibition program focuses on contemporary art, featuring a gallery dedicated to experimental, site-specific, and new media works selected through artist proposals. The various theaters host a wide range of performances, including concerts, dance shows, theater productions, and comedy acts by touring groups and resident companies. With a comprehensive list of courses for adults and children, the Mesa Arts Center offers expert guidance in disciplines such as painting, sculpture, jewelry making, blacksmithing, and acting.

One East Main Street Mesa, Arizona 85201, admin: 480-644-6501, box office: +1 480-644-6500

Tonto National Monument

Situated within the Sonoran Desert, Tonto National Monument is home to impressive cliff dwellings dating back to the 13th century. Visitors can embark on a half-mile hike up a paved trail to explore these fascinating ruins. The national monument not only showcases the architectural marvels of the ancient tribes who inhabited the area but also immerses visitors in the diverse ecosystem of the Sonoran Desert, known for its array of cacti, plants, and wildflowers. The Visitor Center museum displays expertly crafted artifacts left behind by the tribes, offering a glimpse into their daily lives.

26260 N Az Hwy 188 #2 Roosevelt, AZ 85545, +1 928 467-2241

Herberger Theater Center

As the official performance venue for the Arizona Theatre Company and the Center Dance Ensemble, the Herberger Theater Center plays a vital role in Phoenix's cultural scene. Established in 1989 as a non-profit organization, the center aims to expand the city's cultural landscape. It offers a platform for various performance groups, fostering growth in the performing arts. The Herberger Theater Center also operates a youth outreach program, providing young individuals with opportunities to perform on a professional stage and encouraging the future of the arts in Arizona. Additionally, an onsite art gallery sells the work of local artists, with a portion of the proceeds contributing to the theater's development.

222 E Monroe St, Phoenix, AZ 85004, +1 602-254-7399

ASU Art Museum

Reflecting the mentality of Arizona State University, the ASU Art Museum serves as a laboratory for contemplation and inventive artistic engagement. Its projects include 'Global Arizona,' which aims to deepen the connection between art and society, 'Social Studies,' inviting working artists to transform a museum gallery into a studio for visitors to witness their creative process, 'InterLab,' showcasing interdisciplinary work by students and faculty, and 'Moving Targets,' focusing on new media art. Through these initiatives, ASU Art Museum aspires to be a museum of the future.

51 E 10th St, Tempe, AZ 85281, +1 480-965-2787

Phoenix Theatre

Founded in 1924, the Phoenix Theatre is Arizona's oldest arts organization and one of the largest in the United States. Initially established as the permanent venue for the Phoenix Players, the theater has a rich history of presenting the work of emerging playwrights and composers, experimental theater, and world premieres. In the 1950s, the development of a new building for the theater spurred the growth of Phoenix's cultural scene, attracting institutions like the Phoenix Art Museum and the Phoenix Library. The Phoenix Theatre continues to be a hub for artistic expression and creativity.

100 E. McDowell Rd, Phoenix, AZ 85004, +1 602-254-2151

Rock Art Canyon Ranch

Located 13 miles outside Winslow, Rock Art Canyon Ranch offers a unique outdoor art gallery. Visits to this extraordinary site are by appointment only. The ranch showcases an extensive collection of petroglyphs, some of the most remarkable in the state, adorning the canyon walls on either side of a lush stream. In addition to the petroglyphs, the ranch house features hundreds of artifacts collected from the property, creating a convergence of art, nature, and history that provides enlightening insights.

Box 224, Joseph City, AZ 86032, +1 928 288-3260

Modified Arts

Established in 1999, Modified Arts is an innovative exhibition space and performance venue in downtown Phoenix. Its rotating exhibition program presents monthly shows featuring bold, highly conceptual, and diverse works by local, national, and international artists. Alongside visual arts, Modified Arts hosts select musical performances throughout the year, encompassing genres ranging from jazz to contemporary classical to experimental music. The intimate gallery space creates a unique setting for concerts, while performance artists, actors, and dancers are invited to create and perform new works tailored to this distinctive venue.

407 East Roosevelt St. Phoenix, AZ 85004-1918, +1 602 462-5516

Chapter 15: 45 Family-Friendly Activities To Do in Phoenix, Arizona with Kids

Phoenix, Arizona holds a special place in my heart, as it is my hometown. Although I now reside in humid Atlanta, I still consider myself a Phoenician at heart. Thankfully, I have the opportunity to return to the desert at least three times a year to visit family and friends. What's even better is that I now have children of my own, allowing me to rediscover some of my favorite childhood attractions and explore exciting new activities in Phoenix. The city offers an abundance of delightful restaurants, family-friendly entertainment options, and excellent hotels and resorts.

A family vacation in the Valley of the Sun is a perfect getaway, filled with sunshine and endless fun for kids and adults alike. From the luxurious resort spas to the plethora of exciting things to do, Phoenix has something for everyone. Whether you choose to stay in a five-star resort or spend quality time with loved ones, this gem of the Grand Canyon State guarantees a memorable experience.

Phoenix boasts a reliable weather forecast of sunshine, with occasional monsoon seasons. Consequently, there are numerous indoor and outdoor activities to enjoy throughout the year. Don't let the scorching summer temperatures deter you, as most places are equipped with air conditioning, misters, splash pads, and pools. Moreover, visiting during the summer months offers the advantage of lower prices compared to the busier winter season. However, it's crucial to stay hydrated and carry water with you regardless of the season.

Indoor Activities in Phoenix for Kids:

1. LEGOLAND Discovery Center Arizona
Located in Tempe's Arizona Mills Mall, LEGOLAND Discovery Center provides an immersive experience for builders of all ages. Enjoy rides like Kingdom Quest and Merlin's Apprentice, watch a show at Lego 4D Cinema, marvel at the miniature replica of Phoenix crafted entirely from LEGO bricks, climb the giant jungle gym, and immerse yourselves in endless LEGO creations. It's advisable to purchase tickets online in advance to secure your spot, as they tend to sell out quickly.

2. SEA LIFE Arizona Aquarium
Adjacent to LEGOLAND, the SEA LIFE Aquarium promises an equally thrilling adventure. With 250+ species of marine animals across 10 themed zones, this interactive aquarium offers exhibits like Touch Tidepools, a variety of sharks, and a captivating 360-degree ocean tunnel. Keep an eye out for LEGO models amidst the tanks. Combination tickets for LEGOLAND and SEA LIFE are available.

3. Arizona Science Center
Situated in downtown Phoenix, the Arizona Science Center features permanent, hands-on exhibits that engage children of all ages. Explore the CREATE maker space, experience Forces of Nature, and marvel at the

planetarium. The center continually introduces new and fascinating exhibits.

4. Great Arizona Puppet Theater
Enjoy a puppet show at this iconic Phoenix venue, which operates year-round. It's an excellent place to escape the summer heat while being entertained. Recent shows have included favorites like Cinderella and The Three Billy Goats Gruff.

5. Pangaea Land of the Dinosaurs
Become a paleontologist at this interactive dinosaur attraction located at the OdySea Complex. Encounter over 50 life-sized animatronic dinosaurs and explore 10 interactive stations, including a fossil dig, excavation site, and a Dino-Kart ride. It's a must-visit destination for adventure-seeking kids fascinated by dinosaurs. Children aged 2 and under receive free admission. While there, make time to visit the OdySea Aquarium and its impressive two-million-gallon tank, home to sharks and otters.

6. Butterfly Wonderland
Adjacent to Pangaea and OdySea, Butterfly Wonderland offers the largest indoor rainforest conservatory in the United States. Witness over 3,000 butterflies from around the world, along with other bugs and reptiles. With a little patience, you might even have a butterfly land on you. Get your cameras ready for some incredible photo opportunities!

7. Childsplay
As a long-standing family theater, Childsplay has been entertaining children for years. Upcoming shows include The Very Hungry Caterpillar Show and School House Rock Live! Many performances offer backstage tours if reserved in advance.

8. Castles N Coasters
For little adrenaline junkies and thrill seekers, Castles N Coasters is a paradise. This attraction offers an upside-down roller coaster, interactive

experiences, a massive arcade, a log ride, bumper boats, miniature golf, and much more. Food is available for purchase.

9. Children's Museum of Phoenix

The Children's Museum of Phoenix offers endless innovative activities for kids. Explore the art studio, build with blocks, play pretend in the grocery store, construct forts, navigate the Noodle Forest, enjoy the indoor climbing center, and so much more. Families with children of different ages will appreciate the dedicated baby zones within each exhibit, as well as the toddler-friendly furniture and bathroom fixtures. Visit the museum's website to review tip sheets and ensure a fantastic time for everyone.

10. Hall of Flame Fire Museum

Dedicated to all things firefighting, this museum houses an extensive collection. Kids can enjoy the fantastic children's room, complete with a fire pole and a child-sized fire engine equipped with uniforms and protective gear. Visitors of all ages will find pleasure in exploring the museum's array of retro fire trucks.

11. Musical Instrument Museum

The Musical Instrument Museum (MIM) offers a unique experience with its instrument displays, concerts, and drop-in kids' classes. The Geographic Galleries showcase musical instruments from around the world, while the Artist Gallery introduces kids to legendary musicians. The Experience and Encore Galleries provide hands-on interactive music experiences.

12. Jake's Unlimited

Jake's Unlimited is a paradise for kids, featuring amusement rides, laser tag, bowling, an arcade, and more—all under one roof. The "endless eats" option, which includes unlimited food and drinks, ensures a day filled with non-stop fun.

13. Pottery Painting

When the desire to stay cool combines with a burst of creativity, take the kids to paint pottery at As You Wish. With six locations across the Valley, As You Wish provides fully stocked studios and a variety of ready-to-paint creations. Check the online calendar for special events and kid-specific classes.

14. Pinspiration

Pinspiration is a haven for crafty makers. With two locations in the metro area (North Phoenix and Peoria), this Pinterest-inspired DIY art studio and maker space offer a wide selection of project kits. Kids can choose from various activities and tutorials, with reservations suggested to ensure availability.

15. i.d.e.a. Museum

Located in Mesa, the i.d.e.a. Museum focuses on design thinking, project-based learning, and imaginative exploration. It's a wonderful place for children to unleash their creativity and engage in a wide range of activities.

16. Heard Museum

The Heard Museum is a devoted institution celebrating American Indian art. During my childhood, I cherished visiting this museum on field trips and engaging in activities like grinding corn in the atrium. Its remarkable art collection honors the beauty and accomplishments of diverse American Indian tribal cultures throughout the region.

17. iFly

Ever dreamed of experiencing skydiving but felt hesitant about jumping out of a plane? In Scottsdale, you can capture the sensation of flight at iFly. This national chain offers visitors the opportunity to feel like they're flying within a controlled indoor environment, thanks to a unique wind tunnel. Even children as young as 3 can participate.

18. Crayola Experience

Immerse yourself in a world of vibrant colors by visiting the Crayola Experience in Chandler. This lively attraction offers enjoyable activities like personalizing and printing your own crayon wrapper, melting and molding crayons, creating spin art, transforming 2D drawings into animated scenes, and much more.

19. Mirror Maze

Taking a creative twist on the popular escape-room trend, the rainforest-themed Mirror Maze provides an exciting adventure. Explore the jungle, Mayan ruins, and other captivating settings while jungle creatures make intriguing sounds all around you. The lights and mirrors add an element of confusion as you navigate your way out. It's a fantastic way to beat the heat on a hot day and have some fun.

Outdoor Activities in Phoenix for Kids:

20. Phoenix Zoo

Delight in a day at the local zoo, where lions, tigers, bears, and more will entertain your family. If you visit during the warmer months, remember to pack bathing suits for the kids to enjoy the splash pads, which are open from March through October. Don't forget to make a reservation and bring some cash to purchase lettuce for giraffe-feeding times.

21. Pueblo Grande Museum

Located outdoors on a 1,500-year-old archeological site left by the Hohokam, the Pueblo Grande Museum offers a fascinating glimpse into history. The museum itself is of manageable size, suitable for walkers of all abilities. Explore replicated dwellings and learn about the history and culture of the Hohokam people. If you visit during the summer, be sure to bring an umbrella for shade. Admission is free for children under 6, and all kids 17 and under can enter for free on Sundays.

22. McCormick-Stillman Railroad Park

A visit to the McCormick-Stillman Railroad Park in Scottsdale is a must for kids of all ages. Enjoy a ride on a vintage train and a classic carousel. Kids can also explore the train museum and operate miniature train sets using circuits that replicate the city of Phoenix. Additionally, the park features playgrounds and is an excellent venue for hosting birthday parties.

23. Enchanted Island Amusement Park
Spend an entire day at Enchanted Island in Encanto Park, where you'll find a wide range of rides and attractions suitable for all ages. Younger kids can enjoy bumper boats, a carousel, train rides, and more, while older kids can experience thrilling rides like the spin ride and parachute tower. Pedal boats and canoes are available for rental as well.

24. Hurricane Harbor Phoenix
Cool off and have a blast at Arizona's largest water park. You'll find high-speed water slides for thrill-seekers and plenty of family-friendly fun. The park offers a large wave pool, a lazy river, and a designated splash area for little kids featuring pint-sized versions of some of the park's thrilling rides. Hurricane Harbor opens its season in March.

25. Desert Botanical Garden
Immerse yourself in the beauty of the Desert Botanical Garden, filled with an impressive array of cacti and other desert plants. The garden covers a vast area and features plants of varying heights, flowering desert species, and wildflowers, thoughtfully spread across five trails. With more than 50,000 plants, it's a captivating experience. Choose a trail based on your group's abilities, desired duration, or specific interests. Some trails even feature native peoples' housing replicas for kids to explore or take a break. Remember to bring water, sunscreen, hats, and sunglasses, and note that many trails are stroller-friendly.

26. Camelback Mountain
Take advantage of Arizona's mountainous terrain and embark on a hiking adventure. While there are excellent hiking opportunities throughout the

city, Camelback Mountain is renowned for its breathtaking views. Keep in mind that the trails are somewhat challenging, so it's recommended for older children and experienced hikers. Don't forget to bring water, sunscreen, and keep an eye out for wildlife, including rattlesnakes.

27. Splash Pads
Escape the sweltering heat and enjoy spring and summer at splash pads, which offer a refreshing and entertaining experience. These water playgrounds, available for free or at affordable prices, are perfect for cooling off. Your kids will likely dry off by the time you reach the car. Don't miss the splash pad at CityScape or the pop-jet fountain at Scottsdale Quarter.

28. Pioneer Living History Museum
Transport yourself back in time at the Pioneer Living History Museum, an open-air museum spanning 90 acres in north Phoenix. This immersive experience allows visitors to step into an 1800s town, complete with a jail, blacksmith shop, ranch complex, and more, providing a taste of the Wild West. Costumed interpreters breathe life into the pioneer lifestyle.

29. Cactus League Baseball
If you're fortunate enough to visit during MLB's annual spring training, catch a baseball game or two. The Cactus League features 10 stadiums where many MLB teams practice leading up to opening day. These stadiums offer a more intimate experience compared to their regular-season counterparts, making it an enjoyable outing for families with young kids. Some stadiums even have special children's areas to enhance the experience.

30. Other Sports
Phoenix is a paradise for sports lovers, whether your children enjoy baseball, basketball, football, golf, tennis, or other sports. Depending on the time of year, you can catch a Diamondbacks, Cardinals, or Suns game. The city is renowned for its exceptional golf courses and tennis courts, so

take advantage of the opportunity to play and don't forget to bring your equipment.

31. Deer Valley Petroglyph Preserve
Embark on a journey through time and witness one of the Valley of the Sun's largest collections of prehistoric petroglyphs. A leisurely walk along the path will lead you to clearly marked rock art. Enjoy the free audio tour along the trail for a more immersive experience and deeper understanding of the preserve.

32. Go Swimming
Swimming is not just a luxury but a necessity in Phoenix, especially during the scorching summer months. The city offers numerous public pools where you and your kids can cool off and have a splashing good time, free of charge.

33. Golfland Sunsplash
When the Arizona heat becomes intense, there's nothing better than jumping into a pool. But at Golfland Sunsplash, you'll discover that jumping is just one of the many ways to enter the water. This entertainment complex boasts over 30 rides and attractions, including thrilling water slides. And don't forget to challenge your family to a round of mini-golf!

34. Wildlife World Zoo
Get ready for a wild adventure at the Wildlife World Zoo. Located near Goodyear, this animal park houses a vast collection of exotic and endangered animals. Explore the park and encounter reptiles like saltwater crocodiles and even a white alligator, along with marine animals, fish, and other captivating species.

35. Goldfield Ghost Town
Step back in time and relive the Old West at Goldfield Ghost Town in Apache Junction. The town offers various attractions, including gold panning, horseback riding, mine tours, train rides, and more. When hunger

strikes, head over to the Mammoth Steakhouse and Saloon for a satisfying meal.

Phoenix Restaurants Kids Love:

36. Rustler's Rooste

Immerse yourself in the authentic Arizona atmosphere by dining at Rustler's Rooste. Enjoy a steak surrounded by whiskey barrels and wagon wheels while the Lil' Wranglers in your family will be thrilled to discover the indoor slide. With nightly live music and delicious food, Rustler's Rooste is not only a restaurant but also a fantastic Western venue for hosting private events and parties.

37. Peter Piper Pizza

Growing up in Phoenix in the '80s, every kid knew the catchy jingle and "come on over" slogan of Peter Piper Pizza. It has always been the go-to place for hosting birthday parties or hanging out after school. Besides serving delicious pizza, Peter Piper locations offer a variety of entertainment options such as arcade games, indoor playgrounds, carousels, and more (each location has its unique features).

38. Organ Stop Pizza

Who can resist the combination of mouthwatering pizza and a spectacular pipe organ performance? Organ Stop Pizza (OSP) features talented musicians playing The Mighty Wurlitzer (the "O" in OSP), providing delightful entertainment for the audience.

39. Sugar Bowl

Since my childhood, I've been a regular visitor to the vibrant pink ice cream parlor known as Sugar Bowl. Even today, Phoenix kids continue to enjoy the refreshing treats offered at Sugar Bowl. Located in Old Town Scottsdale, Sugar Bowl has been a state landmark since 1958, renowned for serving delicious ice cream in delicate glass dishes. Additionally, they offer soups, sandwiches, and salads.

40. The Teapot
If you're in need of a caffeine fix while your little one burns off some energy, head to The Teapot in downtown Phoenix. This charming coffee shop serves lattes and muffins for the adults and features a spacious outdoor play area for children. The Teapot is also a popular venue for hosting birthday parties and private events. Please note that due to Covid, The Teapot has temporarily closed its public-facing shop.

Family-Friendly Hotels in Phoenix and Surrounding Areas:

41. Hyatt Regency Gainey Ranch
The luxurious Gainey Ranch offers something for everyone. Adults can indulge in the state-of-the-art spa and enjoy the swim-up bar, while youngsters can have a blast with a rock-climbing wall and a massive water playground. The resort boasts over 10 pools, including a sand beach, a 30-foot-tall waterslide, numerous water spouts and fountains, and four plunge pools.

42. Hilton Phoenix Resort at the Peak
When visiting Phoenix, cooling off is essential during the summer and simply enjoyable in the winter. Dive into a stylish experience at this resort, formerly known as Pointe Hilton Squaw Peak Resort. This all-suite hotel features River Ranch, a four-acre water park with water slides, a lazy river, water features, and more.

43. Great Wolf Lodge Arizona
Situated in Scottsdale, Great Wolf Lodge is a resort designed with kids in mind. With an abundance of kid-friendly amenities, you may never want to leave the premises. Enjoy the signature indoor water playground, a ropes course, an interactive MagiQuest scavenger hunt, mini golf, dance parties, and much more. During the winter months, the Lodge offers Snowland, a delightful winter-themed experience.

44. The Wigwam
Located in the West Valley, The Wigwam is a kid-friendly hotel in Phoenix. Guests can enjoy three outdoor pools, water slides, lawn games, live music, and a classic Southwestern ambiance. Depending on the time of your visit, there are plenty of events for kids, such as character breakfasts and live animal presentations.

45. Arizona Grand Resort & Spa
Arizona Grand is an exquisite all-suite hotel that will captivate children with its seven-acre water park, known as Oasis. The park features eight-story tall water slides, a wave pool, a side-by-side lazy river, a spacious hot tub, and Wild Cat Springs, a gentler area perfect for younger kids. It's worth mentioning that Rustler's Rooste, the restaurant mentioned above, is located within the resort.

Chapter 16: Best Things to Do in Arizona with Kids

Most individuals who haven't been to Arizona are likely familiar with two aspects of the state: cacti and the Grand Canyon. However, Arizona has so much more to offer in terms of family-friendly activities and attractions. Whether you're seeking natural beauty, urban entertainment, or breathtaking national parks, Arizona has it all. We've compiled a comprehensive list of the best places to visit in Arizona, including historical sites, baseball experiences, and thrilling adventures set in awe-inspiring locations.

Explore Ancient Native Cultures at Montezuma Castle During Your Arizona Family Vacation

With over 250,000 Native Americans residing within Arizona's borders, native culture plays a significant role in the state. The National Park system diligently preserves much of the ancient culture.

Casa Grande Ruins National Monument, situated between Phoenix and Tucson, safeguards the ruins of the Hohokam people from the 13th century.

Montezuma Castle National Monument, located near Sedona, protects 800-year-old cliff dwellings and is a must-see when visiting the area.

Both Wupatki and Walnut Canyon National Monuments near Flagstaff made our list of the top things to do in Flagstaff with kids. Flagstaff is also home to exceptional cabins for a mountain getaway.

For the best Native American museum experience in the United States, head to Phoenix's Heard Museum. It showcases ten galleries filled with American Indian art and artifacts. Kids can participate in hands-on activities like crafting Yaqui-inspired paper flowers or designing a bandolier bag.

Embark on a Horseback Riding Adventure at McDonald's Ranch

When Arizona was initially settled by Americans, it was a rugged and untamed frontier. Legends like Wyatt Earp and Doc Holliday called the silver boom town of Tombstone home in the 1880s and were part of the legendary gunfight at the OK Corral.

Nowadays, Tombstone is a much safer and family-friendly destination. Visitors can enjoy a mine tour, explore historic buildings and cemeteries, and witness Wild West shows at the original OK Corral.

If you're looking for Western-style fun in the Valley of the Sun, Rawhide Western Town in Chandler offers a range of entertainment and activities. Alternatively, consider kid-friendly horseback riding at McDonald's Ranch in North Scottsdale.

Exploring Arizona's ghost towns is another captivating way to immerse yourself in the state's past. Here are some of the best ghost towns to visit in Arizona:

1. Jerome: Located in central Arizona, Jerome is one of the most famous and well-preserved ghost towns in the state. Once a booming copper mining town, it now boasts a vibrant arts community, historical buildings, and stunning views of the Verde Valley. Explore the old mining structures, visit the Jerome State Historic Park, and enjoy the town's unique atmosphere.

2. Tombstone: Known as "The Town Too Tough to Die," Tombstone is an iconic ghost town in southern Arizona. It rose to prominence during the silver mining boom in the late 1800s and is infamous for the legendary gunfight at the O.K. Corral. Stroll along Allen Street, visit the historic buildings, and watch reenactments of the Old West in this lively ghost town.

3. Ruby: Tucked away in the remote desert near the Mexican border, Ruby is a well-preserved ghost town that offers a glimpse into Arizona's mining past. Once a thriving mining town, it now stands as a silent testament to its former glory. Take a guided tour to explore the remaining structures and learn about the town's fascinating history.

4. Oatman: Located on Route 66 in western Arizona, Oatman is a quirky ghost town with a lively twist. Known for its resident wild burros that roam the streets, Oatman has a charming old-west ambiance. Explore the historic buildings, enjoy the western-themed shops, and watch the daily gunfight reenactments.

5. Goldfield: Situated near Apache Junction in the Superstition Mountains, Goldfield is a reconstructed ghost town that offers a glimpse into Arizona's gold rush era. Experience the Old West through the town's historic buildings, gold mine tours, and a narrow-gauge train ride. Don't miss the mesmerizing views of the surrounding desert and the Superstition Mountains.

6. Fairbank: Nestled along the San Pedro River in southeastern Arizona, Fairbank was once a crucial supply hub during the mining boom. Now a ghost town, it offers a peaceful and haunting experience. Explore the old schoolhouse, the cemetery, and the visitor center, which provides insight into the town's history and the surrounding nature.

Remember, when visiting these ghost towns, it's important to respect the historic sites and natural surroundings. Take only photographs and leave no trace behind. Additionally, some ghost towns may require a small fee for entry or have limited facilities, so it's advisable to plan ahead.

Experience Family Fun in Arizona's Sonoran Desert
A significant portion of Arizona is desert, with the iconic Saguaro cactus serving as the state's most renowned symbol. One of the best activities in Arizona is visiting Saguaro National Park.

Stretching across both sides of Tucson, the park not only safeguards a crucial ecosystem but also offers families a chance to truly immerse themselves in the desert environment.

Late winter or early spring is the ideal time to explore the park. The temperatures are mild, wildflowers are in full bloom, and desert hikes are less likely to result in heat exhaustion.

If you visit in June, you'll witness the short-lived blooms of the Saguaro cacti. For an excellent stay in Tucson, we recommend the JW Marriott Tucson Star Pass Resort.

For desert exploration near Phoenix, consider a day hike up Pinnacle Peak or a visit to the Phoenix Mountain Preserve.

During the warmer months, a relaxing float down the chilly Salt River is hard to beat. The Apache Trail is another popular desert drive that offers families a genuine desert adventure with remarkable vistas.

Visit Kid-Friendly Museums in Arizona

Located just south of Saguaro National Park, The Arizona-Sonora Desert Museum showcases the wonders of the Sonoran Desert. Combining elements of a zoo, botanical garden, and natural history museum, the museum seamlessly blends its animal enclosures into the desert landscape.

As families stroll along the trail, they'll spot coyotes peeking out from behind Saguaro cacti, javelinas sauntering past silvery agave plants, and Ferruginous Hawks soaring above. The museum boasts 140 different cacti and other desert plants.

Make sure to explore the hummingbird aviary, Cat Canyon, and a cave that provides a glimpse into the subterranean world.

Don't miss the Musical Instrument Museum in Phoenix, where you can see and hear musical instruments from around the globe. The Experience Gallery is particularly enjoyable for kids of all ages, as they can play various instruments from different cultures.

Another fantastic option for family fun is the Arizona Science Center in Phoenix. With over 350 interactive exhibits, kids can immerse themselves in learning about topics ranging from the human body to electricity.

Located just a 3-minute walk from the Science Center, the Children's Museum of Phoenix offers indoor play opportunities, especially during the scorching summer months. Geared towards younger children (ages 1-10), the museum focuses on learning through play. Kids love exploring the Noodle Forest, engaging in Block Mania, and experiencing the Market, where they can play grocery shopping like mom and dad.

Enjoy America's Favorite Pastime during Spring Training
Every March, thousands of fans flock to Arizona to watch their favorite major league teams during pre-season baseball games. Spring Training games are relaxed, affordable, and perfect for families.

The smaller Cactus League stadiums often have grassy areas behind the outfield, providing ideal spaces for little ones to stretch their legs between innings. The laid-back atmosphere encourages players to sign autographs and interact with enthusiastic kids.

Take a Train Ride
It's no secret that kids and trains are a perfect match. Train enthusiasts will be thrilled to know that Arizona offers plenty of railroad-themed activities.

McCormick-Stillman Railroad Park in Scottsdale is a paradise for train-loving kids. Visitors can ride on the Paradise and Pacific Railroad, explore an expansive indoor model train display, and enjoy a carousel and two large playgrounds (one of which is shaded).

For a unique Arizonan experience, hop aboard the Verde Canyon Railroad or the Grand Canyon Railway in Northern Arizona. Both railways feature classic train cars and breathtaking views. The 2.5-hour journey on the Grand Canyon Railway is filled with entertainment, including a Wild West shootout and roaming actors and musicians performing in a frontier-style manner.

Cool Off at Arizona's Desert Lakes
There's no denying that Arizona summers can be scorching hot! Fortunately, the state boasts several lakes perfect for camping, boating, and, of course, swimming. Lake Havasu, situated on the California-Arizona border, is a popular destination for water sports enthusiasts.

In addition to enjoying jet skiing, water skiing, and tubing, be sure to visit the original London Bridge. This historic landmark once spanned the River Thames in England before being dismantled in the late 1960s and brought to Lake Havasu City.

Houseboaters adore Lake Powell in the Glen Canyon National Recreation Area, a narrow lake boasting numerous serene coves surrounded by stunning painted desert canyons and mesas. Don't miss the chance to visit Rainbow Bridge, the largest natural arch in the world, accessible by boat and a 1-mile hike from the lake.

After exploring Lake Powell, make sure to visit the nearby Antelope Canyon in the Lake Powell Navajo Tribal Park, famous for its enchanting sandstone formations. Iconic Horseshoe Bend is also in close proximity, offering fantastic photo opportunities. However, exercise caution and keep a close eye on children near the edge.

Spend a Day in Phoenix's Papago Park
Papago Park is a must-visit destination for those traveling to Phoenix. Families can enjoy picnic areas, small fishing lakes, hiking trails, and

bicycle paths. The prominent sandstone butte known as Hole in the Rock provides magnificent views of the city.

Within the park lies the Desert Botanical Garden, an expansive 145-acre garden home to over 50,000 desert plants. It offers various programs geared towards kids, including the interactive Cacti Quest that combines desert ecology, map reading, nature observation, and adventure for children aged 8 and up.

The Phoenix Zoo is another popular attraction within Papago Park. While many visitors explore the zoo on foot, you can also bring your bikes and ride from exhibit to exhibit, adding an extra layer of fun to your zoo experience. Enjoy the Arizona Trail, Monkey Village, Giraffe Encounter, pedal boats, Safari Train, petting zoo, and a playful playground with a Saguaro cactus-shaped slide.

Experience the Red Rocks of Sedona
They say, "God created the Grand Canyon, but he lives in Sedona." Sedona is renowned for its special energy and is worth staying in for a few days to truly soak it in. The breathtaking red rocks leave a lasting impression on those fortunate enough to experience their splendor.

Embark on an off-road adventure with Pink Jeep Tours, taking your family to destinations like Diamondback Gulch and Chicken Point. Knowledgeable guides provide insights into local history, geology, and native culture.

For those eager to stretch their legs, hiking in Red Rock State Park offers numerous fascinating rock formations to explore and climb upon.

If you're seeking a thrilling water experience, Slide Rock State Park is the perfect destination. Whiz down the natural water chutes and enjoy a day of excitement.

Don't miss day trips to Montezuma Castle and Casa Grande National Monuments or a visit to Out of Africa Wildlife Park, where you can feed giraffes and tigers.

Visit the Grand Canyon
Few places rival the iconic status of the Grand Canyon. The views from both the North Rim and South Rim are breathtaking and offer different perspectives. The North Rim provides a more remote and wooded experience compared to the South Rim.

Trekaroo has a comprehensive guide to the Grand Canyon South Rim with kids, as well as a detailed guide to the Grand Canyon North Rim.

For an ultimate whitewater adventure, ride the Colorado River rapids in a dorie. Active families will find the journey to the stunningly blue Havasu Falls, located on the Havasupai Indian Reservation, to be a popular and rewarding experience. If you prefer a more leisurely pace, the Grand Canyon Rim Trail offers stunning views and opportunities to spot wildlife.

Flagstaff, a charming western town, serves as the gateway to the Grand Canyon. While the park offers camping and lodges, more comfortable accommodations can be found in Flagstaff.

If you're seeking an epic hike in the Grand Canyon, consider the trail along Havasu Creek leading to Havasu Falls.

7. Hidden Gems and Off-the-Beaten-Path
   - Lesser-Known National Parks and Monuments
   - Secret Canyons and Hidden Waterfalls
   - Ghost Towns and Historic Mines
   - Unique Natural Formations
   - Quirky Roadside Attractions

Chapter 17: The Hidden Gems and Secret Places of Northern Arizona

Embark on a unique and memorable trip in northern Arizona by exploring these secret places that offer a break from the crowds and a chance to connect with the state's wild landscapes.

Before you set off, it's important to note that many of these attractions are spread out and sometimes located in remote areas. To make the most of your journey, we recommend bringing your own car or renting one, preferably with four-wheel drive.

Discover Peach Springs, a small town on Route 66, known as the base camp for adventure in northern Arizona. Explore the underground accommodations or experience the Skywalk, a thrilling opportunity to float above the Grand Canyon. This quaint capital of the Hualapai Nation offers a range of exciting activities.

Visit the Grand Canyon Caverns, a treasure trove of family fun. These caverns were discovered in 1927 and have a fascinating history, including the remains of a giant sloth that went extinct thousands of years ago. Take a tour, including a ghost tour, and enjoy lunch 200 feet underground at the Cavern Grill. Don't miss the chance to sleep in the "master suite" after the ghost tour for a truly memorable experience.

Embark on a journey to Rock Art Ranch, accessible via Rock Art Ranch Road. This hidden gem, a working cattle ranch, is rarely visited by out-of-towners. Contact the owner, Brantley Baird, who has lived on the ranch since 1948, and take a personalized tour of his home. Explore ancient petroglyphs, ruins, and a small museum displaying American Indian and pioneer artifacts.

Uncover the history of the Apache Death Cave, a fascinating and spooky location on Route 66 between Flagstaff and Winslow. In 1878, over 40 Apache Indians were discovered hiding underground in this cavern during a series of conflicts with the Navajo tribesmen. The cave and surrounding area are considered cursed and haunted, making it an intriguing destination for brave visitors.

While The Wave, a famous rock formation, may be well-known, don't overlook the other wonders of Vermilion Cliffs National Monument. This 280,000-acre monument nestled between Kaibab National Forest and Glen Canyon National Recreation Area offers stunning views and the opportunity to spot endangered California condors. Explore this special place that beckons to adventurous travelers, remembering that permits are required for The Wave and can be obtained through a lottery system.

For a unique accommodation experience, stay at the Shash Dine Eco Retreat near Page. This traditional Navajo hogan, known as the "5 Billion Star Hotel," is beautifully crafted with earth and logs. Located on a working sheep ranch in the Navajo Nation, it offers proximity to popular destinations like Antelope Canyon, Horseshoe Bend, Lake Powell, and the Grand Canyon.

Embark on the Arizona Hot Spring Trail, a 5-mile round trip accessible only by foot. This remote hot spring near Lake Mead provides a quiet retreat in a tranquil natural setting. Enjoy a rewarding plunge into the hot spring after walking along a rocky arroyo towards the Colorado River. Visit the official Arizona Hot Spring Trail website for safety precautions and route-finding information.

For a family-friendly stop, Delgadillo's Snow Cap Drive-In in Seligman is a perfect choice. This historic eatery and roadside attraction, built from scrap lumber in 1953, offers a dose of nostalgia and a humorous menu. Stop by for an iconic photo and a fun pit stop.

Escape the city lights and enjoy stargazing at the Dome Stargazing House in Williams. Although not officially designated as an International Dark Sky Community, Williams has significantly less light pollution than many other cities.

Include a visit to Mystery Valley while exploring Monument Valley Navajo Tribal Park. Located near the town of Kayenta in the Navajo Nation, this remote desert area resembles another world. Explore ancient indigenous ruins, petroglyphs, and a landscape teeming with life. Remember that a guide is required to explore this sacred area, and you can find one at the Monument Valley Visitor Center.

Take a historical detour at the Burger King in Kayenta, where a small museum pays tribute to the Navajo Code Talkers. These brave Navajo men developed an unbreakable code during World War II, using their complex and unwritten language for communication in the United States Marines. This display is a must-see for travelers passing through northern Arizona.

Experience a journey back in time with a stay at the Homesteader Cabin in Fredonia, just south of the Utah border. This historic cabin, equipped with modern comforts, offers solitude and an authentic Wild West retreat. It's an ideal location for those traveling between Zion and Grand Canyon National Parks or seeking a unique off-the-beaten-path experience.

Finally, don't miss the North Rim of the Grand Canyon, a hidden gem that offers a quieter and cooler alternative to the popular South Rim. With stunning views and access, the North Rim provides a remote adventure just a short distance from its southern counterpart. Keep in mind that the North Rim is closed during the winter and reopens around mid-May.

Chapter 18: Best Kept Secrets In Arizona

When thoughts of Arizona come to mind, certain images are likely to surface: The Grand Canyon, Saguaro cacti, hot summers, golf, and hiking.

And you're absolutely right. These are all well-known aspects of Arizona that make it a fantastic destination, as nearly 44 million people would agree.

While we appreciate these popular highlights that make Arizona a hot spot, we also enjoy discovering hidden gems that haven't been explored by millions each year. There's a certain thrill in venturing off the beaten path and experiencing something that gets your adrenaline pumping, don't you think?

That's why we've made it our mission to unveil some of Arizona's best-kept secrets, inviting you to visit them before they become the next big thing in the Grand Canyon State.

LOCAL ARIZONA SECRETS YOU'LL ADORE

1. THE WAVE

Unearthing this secret requires some effort, but we assure you it's worth it. By "effort," we mean participating in a lottery almost five months ahead of your planned trip, hoping to secure a coveted hiking permit from the Bureau of Land Management.

Alternatively, if you're feeling more adventurous or didn't plan ahead, you can try your luck in-person and hope to be one of the fortunate 20 individuals granted entry.

Before the challenge of gaining access deters you from this secret spot, let us share some information about the Wave. Nestled on the Utah border within the Paria Canyon Wilderness Area, it is unlike anything you've ever seen or will see again.

The red sandstone structures forming the Wave were shaped through the calcification of rocks in both horizontal and vertical directions, resulting in a distinctive patterned appearance. Exploring these breathtaking views will leave you feeling exhilarated, especially given the exclusivity that ensures minimal foot traffic on the trail.

2. MONTEZUMA CASTLE

As one of the most remarkably preserved cliff dwellings in the country, Montezuma Castle is well worth a visit.

This architectural wonder dates back to the 12th century when the Sinagua Indians constructed this massive castle within the rocks. They expertly carved out nearly 20 rooms spanning five stories, all facing south to capture the sun's warmth for heating the living spaces.

Despite its name suggesting otherwise, this castle is not affiliated with Aztec culture. The name was a result of European settlers mistaking its origin.

As one of the world's first national monuments, Montezuma Castle is a captivating sight to behold.

3. ARCOSANTI

Architect Paolo Soleri initiated this extraordinary project in the middle of what seemed like nowhere, driven by a vision to create an urban development where people could thrive without harming Mother Nature.

He coined this concept "arcology."

While the space hasn't fully realized Soleri's initial aspirations, it still thrives in its own unique way here in Arizona. Visitors can drop by to witness the sustainable living arrangements and gain insights into the lives of Arcosanti's residents. Don't miss the collection of remarkable bells, designed by Soleri himself, which draw crowds from all over.

Arcosanti features several apartments, a beautiful visitor center, a swimming pool, and an outdoor auditorium as part of its development.

Take a fascinating look into an alternative way of living.

4. MOUNT GRAHAM INTERNATIONAL OBSERVATORY

Welcome the world's largest telescope in Safford, Arizona, which can actually outperform the renowned Hubble Space Telescope.

This colossal telescope was constructed at the Steward Observatory Mirror Lab, one of the few places on Earth capable of building such a marvel. The Large Binocular Telescope (LBT) consists of two 27-foot-long mirrors weighing nearly 2 tons each.

During your Arizona trip, embark on a weekend tour that takes you up Mount Graham to witness this impressive sight up close. Along the way, you'll learn not only about the telescope but also about the mountain and its other wonders.

5. PETRIFIED NATIONAL FOREST NATIONAL PARK

At first, the idea of visiting a place where ancient trees once thrived may not sound particularly thrilling.

However, these are not ordinary trees. These petrified remains date back over 218 million years. Yes, you read that correctly—218 MILLION YEARS. It's difficult to fathom something so ancient, especially considering that remnants of it still exist today.

Some of the trees are mere fragments, while others are massive, 6-foot-wide specimens.

Immerse yourself in history at Petrified Forest National Park and witness more than just remnants of old trees. The park also showcases geological formations and ancient art, fulfilling any archaeologist's dreams.

Explore the park by taking one of its fairly easy and family-friendly hiking trails, keeping in mind that shade is scarce, and the sun can be intense.

If time is limited, the National Park Service has created sample itineraries offering guidance based on the available time you have.

6. SECRET CANYON

We adore a hidden spot with the word "secret" in its name, especially when it can be mistaken for its more popular and overcrowded counterpart, Antelope Canyon.

Undoubtedly, you've seen stunning photos of Antelope Canyon. It's impossible to take a bad picture when surrounded by such awe-inspiring scenery. However, due to its fame, Antelope Canyon can become overwhelmingly crowded.

Thankfully, we've discovered an excellent Plan B: Secret Canyon. With a maximum of only 15 people at a time, you'll enjoy an intimate exploration of this breathtaking canyon, capturing photographs without the risk of unwanted intrusions.

While the price may be slightly higher than Antelope Canyon, we firmly believe the tranquility and personal experience make it worthwhile.

7. CAVE OF THE BELLS

Touring a cave is always an exciting endeavor, but imagine adding an extra level of excitement and exclusivity by requiring a key for entry.

Due to its delicate nature, Cave of the Bells is an underground wilderness area safeguarded by a literal key. While there's no fee to access the caves, a key deposit is required.

Rest assured, the experience is well worth it. Unlike other caves, as you venture deeper, the temperature actually rises. The most popular passageway, Lake Tunnel, leads to an underground lake with water temperatures reaching nearly 80 degrees!

Both seasoned spelunkers and beginners will relish this exploration. However, it is vital to bear in mind the fragility of the area and exercise caution with every step you take.

8. SUNSET CRATER NATIONAL MONUMENT

For a glimpse into history, make your way to Sunset Crater National Monument. This area was once a dormant volcano that erupted almost 1000 years ago, leaving behind a dark spot on the landscape. Over the following centuries, the volcano continued to erupt, shaping the unique Arizona scenery you see today.

You can still witness the remnants of the volcano's lava, frozen in stone. The trail through the crater offers breathtaking views and leads to the Ice Cave lava tube. If you have time, there are several other trails in the area worth exploring.

9. WATSON LAKE

Arizona is home to several beautiful lakes, each with its own charm. Among them, Watson Lake stands out as a hidden gem with fewer visitors. Located near Prescott, this lake boasts stunning granite dells that provide picturesque backdrops and opportunities for leisurely walks and exploration.

There is no shortage of activities to enjoy at Watson Lake. From fishing to hiking, rock climbing to kayaking, you'll find a day's worth of fun waiting for you.

Now, you have a fantastic mix of well-known tourist attractions and off-the-beaten-path destinations to discover on your next trip to Arizona. With its diverse offerings, the Grand Canyon State invites you to take your time and immerse yourself in all the excitement it has to offer.

Chapter 19: Hidden Gems in Arizona No Family Should Miss

Arizona, known for the remarkable Grand Canyon, is also home to numerous hidden treasures that will captivate families. From enigmatic castles and caverns to ghost towns and mesmerizing chocolate waterfalls, the state offers a plethora of off-the-beaten-path destinations.

While Grand Canyon National Park is an undeniable must-see attraction, embarking on a road trip to this renowned site presents an opportunity to uncover Arizona's hidden gems.

Referred to as the "Grand Canyon State," Arizona ranks as the sixth largest state, boasting a remarkably diverse landscape and an abundance of natural wonders. Visitors can explore parks, lakes, rock formations, cacti-dotted landscapes, sandstone canyons, and pine forests. History enthusiasts and outdoor adventurers alike will find plenty to explore by foot or car, including a section of the iconic Route 66.

Indulge in the beauty of Grand Falls, also known as the "Chocolate Waterfalls." These striking waterfalls derive their nickname from the rich, brown color resulting from the sediment of the Little Colorado River. Located in the Leupp Chapter of the Navajo Nation, approximately 30 miles northeast of Flagstaff, Grand Falls offers a unique and captivating natural phenomenon. The 90-minute roundtrip drive from Interstate 40 at Winona is well worth the effort. Additionally, Grand Falls is conveniently accessible from Grand Canyon National Park and Petrified Forest National Park, situated within a four-hour drive from Phoenix.

To experience the red-sand desert region, venture on the looping 17-mile Valley Drive through Monument Valley. Located at the Arizona-Utah border, this mesmerizing landscape showcases towering sandstone buttes, some exceeding 1,000 feet in height.

Explore the wonders of Kartchner Caverns State Park, a cave system discovered by two young explorers in 1974. Designated as an Arizona State Park in 1988, it opened for public tours in 1999. Various guided tours are available, providing an opportunity to learn about the caves' history. The Kartchner Caverns State Park Discovery Center features hands-on exhibits that further enhance the experience.

Immerse yourself in the fascinating rock formations of Chiricahua National Monument, often referred to as the "Wonderland of Rocks." A picturesque eight-mile paved road leads to a forest of rock spires, complemented by 18 miles of day-use hiking trails. Each twist and turn reveals a new vista adorned with unique shapes and sizes of rocks. Chiricahua National Monument is located 120 miles southeast of Tucson.

While the wave-like sandstone structures of the Paria Wilderness, aptly called The Wave, are not accessible, their distinctive beauty can still be admired. Located north of the Grand Canyon's North Rim, these formations are composed of Navajo Sandstone dunes that have solidified into compacted rocks through vertical and horizontal calcification.

Delve into the history of Mystery Castle, an extraordinary desert structure. Built in the 1930s by Boyce Luther Gulley for his daughter Mary Lou Gulley, this castle stands as a testament to Gulley's love and determination. Constructed from an assortment of building materials, it features 18 rooms and 13 fireplaces. The castle remained unknown to Gulley's wife and daughter until his passing in 1945. Since then, it has become a popular tourist attraction.

At Bearizona Drive-Through Zoo in Williams, families can observe bison, wolves, rocky mountain goats, and other North American wildlife from the comfort and safety of their own vehicles. The three-mile drive-through route winds through a Ponderosa pine forest, offering an up-close encounter with over 50 species, including black bears, jaguars, and bobcats, living in their natural environments. More than half of the animals residing at the safari park were rescued.

Out of Africa Wildlife Park in Camp Verde provides an opportunity to meet and learn about rescued animals, such as Boom Boom the rhino and Vista the Bengal Tiger. The park's focus on conservation makes it a home for numerous endangered species. Visitors can enjoy interactive experiences like feeding a tiger and feeling a sloth's hair, as well as soaring above the animals on the Predator Zipline. Verde Ranch RV Resort offers the unique experience of spending the night in a western-themed Conestoga covered wagon.

Immerse yourself in the Arizona-Sonora Desert Museum in Tucson, a sprawling institution encompassing a museum, zoo, and gardens. Designed to provide a natural habitat for wildlife, the museum offers a wide range of attractions, including hiking trails, petroglyphs, wildlife viewing opportunities, and ever-changing exhibits. With each visit, families are bound to discover something new in this vast desert oasis.

Watson Lake in Prescott is a hidden gem characterized by its striking striated rock formations. While swimming is not allowed, visitors can engage in activities like fishing, boating, canoeing, kayaking, hiking, rock climbing, camping, and picnicking, all against the backdrop of this captivating natural wonder.

Page is not only a gateway to the majestic Lake Powell but is also home to Horseshoe Bend, a natural wonder also known as Secret Canyon. While other slot canyons near Antelope Canyon tend to be crowded, Horseshoe Bend offers a thrilling and less crowded experience. Take a slot canyon tour, suitable for all ages, and ride in an open-air vehicle from Page to Horseshoe Bend Slot Canyon, located on Navajo land. These tours provide excitement and breathtaking views of the red rock formations. It's advisable to wear closed-toe shoes due to the hot sand.

Uncover the remnants of an authentic ghost town at Castle Dome Ghost Town, located approximately 30 minutes outside of Yuma. This restored 1860s silver mining town showcases mining equipment and over 50 buildings, including a bank, jail, blacksmith, inn, and church. Many artifacts found in the Castle Dome mining district are on display, offering a glimpse into the area's history.

Visit Montezuma Castle National Monument in Sedona, where a self-guided trail leads to a remarkable 1,000-year-old high-rise dwelling. The Sinagua cliff dwelling stands five stories tall with 50 rooms, providing a fascinating glimpse into the past. While there, consider exploring Montezuma Well, where additional cliff dwellings, pueblo ruins, and a pithouse can be found.

In Saguaro National Park near Tucson, hike the Signal Hill trail to enjoy desert views and encounter impressive petroglyphs estimated to be over 1,000 years old. This popular 0.3-mile trail attracts hikers, birding enthusiasts, and horseback riders. The park also features a vast saguaro cactus forest that stretches across the valley floor. The Signal Hill picnic area offers tables and shade, and a large petroglyph site lies just north of the picnic area.

For those seeking adventure, the Apache Death Cave in Winslow presents an intriguing and somewhat eerie attraction. Located along the Old Route 66 in Two Guns, this cave has a tragic history associated with an Apache attack on a Navajo settlement in 1878. The site is believed to be cursed by many Native Americans, but it draws thrill-seeking visitors who wish to catch a glimpse of the cave.

For a captivating journey into the Wild West, a visit to Tombstone is an excellent choice. Known for its famous shootout at OK Corral in 1881, this historic town offers a glimpse into the past. Highlights include a gallows replica and a cemetery where local Outlaws are laid to rest.

Arizona, renowned for the awe-inspiring Grand Canyon, holds numerous hidden treasures that will enchant families. From enigmatic castles and mysterious caverns to ghost towns and captivating chocolate waterfalls, the state offers a wide array of off-the-beaten-path destinations.

While the Grand Canyon National Park undoubtedly claims the spotlight, a road trip to this famous site presents an opportunity to uncover Arizona's lesser-known gems.

Often referred to as the "Grand Canyon State," Arizona stands as the sixth largest state, boasting a remarkably diverse landscape and an abundance of natural wonders. Visitors can explore parks, lakes, rock formations, cacti-studded landscapes, sandstone canyon walls, and pine forests. History buffs and outdoor adventurers will find plenty to explore on foot or by car, including a section of the iconic Route 66.

Immerse yourself in the captivating beauty of Grand Falls, affectionately known as the "Chocolate Waterfalls." These striking waterfalls owe their name to the rich, brown color derived from the sediment of the Little Colorado River. Located in the Leupp Chapter of the Navajo Nation, approximately 30 miles northeast of Flagstaff, Grand Falls offers a unique and captivating natural phenomenon. The 90-minute roundtrip drive from Interstate 40 at Winona is well worth the effort. Additionally, Grand Falls is conveniently accessible from Grand Canyon National Park and Petrified Forest National Park, situated within a four-hour drive from Phoenix.

To experience the captivating red-sand desert region, embark on the scenic 17-mile Valley Drive through Monument Valley. This breathtaking landscape, situated at the Arizona-Utah border, showcases towering sandstone buttes, some surpassing 1,000 feet in height.

Delve into the wonders of Kartchner Caverns State Park, a cave system discovered by two young explorers in 1974. Designated as an Arizona State Park in 1988, it opened for public tours in 1999. Various guided tours offer an opportunity to delve into the caves' history. The Kartchner Caverns State Park Discovery Center features interactive exhibits that further enhance the experience.

Immerse yourself in the fascinating rock formations of Chiricahua National Monument, often referred to as the "Wonderland of Rocks." An eight-mile paved road leads to a forest of rock spires, complemented by 18 miles of day-use hiking trails. Each twist and turn reveals a new vista adorned with unique shapes and sizes of rocks. Chiricahua National Monument is located 120 miles southeast of Tucson.

While the undulating sandstone structures of the Paria Wilderness, aptly called The Wave, are not accessible, their distinctive beauty can still be admired. Situated north of the Grand Canyon's North Rim, these formations are composed of Navajo Sandstone dunes that have solidified into compacted rocks through vertical and horizontal calcification.

Uncover the secrets of Mystery Castle, an extraordinary desert structure. Constructed in the 1930s by Boyce Luther Gulley for his daughter Mary Lou Gulley, this castle stands as a testament to Gulley's love and determination. Built from a variety of building materials, it features 18 rooms and 13 fireplaces. The castle remained unknown to Gulley's wife and daughter until his passing in 1945. Since then, it has become a popular tourist attraction.

Bearizona Drive-Through Zoo in Williams offers a unique opportunity to observe bison, wolves, rocky mountain goats, and other North American wildlife from the comfort and safety of your own vehicle. The three-mile drive-through route winds through a Ponderosa pine forest, providing an up-close encounter with over 50 species, including black bears, jaguars, and bobcats, thriving in their natural environments. More than half of the animals residing at this safari park were rescued.

In Camp Verde, Out of Africa Wildlife Park introduces visitors to rescued animals, such as Boom Boom the rhino and Vista the Bengal Tiger. With a strong focus on conservation, the park serves as a sanctuary for numerous endangered species. Interactive experiences include feeding a tiger and touching a sloth's hair. Additionally, visitors can soar above the animals on the Predator Zipline. Verde Ranch RV Resort offers a unique lodging experience with western-themed Conestoga covered wagons.

Tucson's Arizona-Sonora Desert Museum invites you to explore its vast museum, zoo, and gardens, designed to provide a natural habitat for wildlife. Hiking trails, petroglyphs, wildlife viewing opportunities, and changing exhibits make it a must-see attraction in the Sonoran desert. With each visit, families are bound to discover something new in this expansive desert oasis.

Prescott's Watson Lake, with its striking striated rock formations, remains one of Arizona's best-kept secrets. While swimming is not permitted, visitors can engage in activities such as fishing, boating, canoeing, kayaking, hiking, rock climbing, camping, and picnicking against the backdrop of this captivating natural wonder.

Page, a gateway to majestic Lake Powell, is also home to Horseshoe Bend, a natural wonder often referred to as Secret Canyon. Unlike the more crowded slot canyons near Antelope Canyon, Horseshoe Bend offers a thrilling and less crowded experience. Slot canyon tours, suitable for all ages, transport visitors in open-air vehicles from Page to Horseshoe Bend

Slot Canyon, located on Navajo land. These tours provide excitement and breathtaking views of the red rock formations. It is advisable to wear closed-toe shoes due to the hot sand.

Castle Dome Ghost Town, situated approximately 30 minutes outside of Yuma, allows visitors to explore an authentic ghost town. Restored to its former glory, this 1860s silver mining town features mining equipment and over 50 buildings, including a bank, jail, blacksmith, inn, and church. Many artifacts discovered in the Castle Dome mining district are on display, offering a glimpse into the area's history.

In Sedona, Montezuma Castle National Monument protects a remarkable 1,000-year-old high-rise dwelling. A self-guided trail leads visitors past the five-story, 50-room Sinagua cliff dwelling. Additionally, Montezuma Well offers opportunities to hike past more cliff dwellings, pueblo ruins, and a pithouse. Built by the Sinagua Indians in the 12th century, it stands as one of the nation's most well-preserved cliff dwellings.

For awe-inspiring desert views and encounters with ancient petroglyphs estimated to be over 1,000 years old, hike the Signal Hill trail in Saguaro National Park near Tucson. Popular among hikers, birding enthusiasts, and horseback riders, this 0.3-mile trail leads to a large petroglyph site. The park's giant saguaro cactus forest, stretching across the valley floor, is another notable feature. Visitors should plan accordingly for the park's scorching summer temperatures and bring ample drinking water.

Adventure seekers can catch a glimpse of Apache Death Cave in Winslow, located along the Old Route 66 in Two Guns, Arizona. This cave holds a tragic history, with legend recounting an Apache attack on a Navajo settlement in 1878. In retaliation, Navajo leaders set fire to the cave, claiming the lives of forty-two Apaches. Many Native Americans believe the land is cursed, but it continues to attract thrill-seekers intrigued by the cave's legacy.

For a journey into the Wild West, Tombstone offers an off-the-beaten path experience. Famous for the historic shootout at OK Corral in 1881, this town allows visitors to immerse themselves in the past. Highlights include a replica gallows and a cemetery where local outlaws rest eternally.

Chapter 20: Explore The Enchanting Petrified Forest National Park

If you're a nature enthusiast, food lover, weekend adventurer, parent, spiritual seeker, or a combination of them all, Arizona offers extraordinary and unforgettable experiences that should be at the top of your dream list.

Thrilling Wilderness Escapades

Embark on the ultimate life-changing wilderness experience by rafting through the awe-inspiring Grand Canyon. With a variety of options available, from motorized expeditions lasting three days to 18-day oar adventures, you can choose the adventure that suits you best. For those who love multiple sports, consider combining whitewater kayaking with a tranquil hike on the Canyon's North Rim. Alternatively, immerse yourself in the artistry of handmade dory boats as you paddle along the Colorado River. If hiking is more your style, head to the western side of the Canyon and trek to the captivating Havasu Falls, where cascading water and teal-hued travertine pools create a paradise-like setting.

Arizona holds a special place in my heart, and with each visit, I continue to discover new and wonderful corners to explore. The state is a treasure trove of history, culture, natural beauty, and relaxation opportunities. One of the best ways to experience the richness of Arizona is by taking a day trip to Sedona from Phoenix. I've been to Sedona twice in the past year, once on a family day trip from Phoenix and another time for a rejuvenating girls' weekend getaway. I've also made numerous visits over the years, and each time, I find something new to love.

Now, while I understand the appeal of planning a weekend or longer stay in Sedona, one of the great things about a day trip from Phoenix to Sedona is its feasibility. The drive typically takes around 90 minutes if you don't make any stops along the way. However, if you need a coffee or breakfast option, I've heard great things about Nora Jeans Koffee Kitchen.

In this chapter on day trips to Sedona, I'll present you with three fantastic options that cater to different types of travelers. Each itinerary is divided into morning and afternoon blocks, allowing you to mix and match to create your perfect day in Sedona. And if you prefer to extend your stay and explore all the wonderful things Sedona has to offer, you can easily combine these options into a weekend itinerary.

Tips for Planning a Day Trip from Phoenix to Sedona

If possible, I recommend renting a car and visiting Sedona on your own instead of booking a tour. This gives you the freedom to enjoy the tranquility of the area and choose which Sedona attractions you want to prioritize, rather than adhering to a fixed schedule or someone else's preferences.

While traffic on the 115-mile drive from Phoenix to Sedona is usually manageable, I suggest leaving early on weekends just in case. On weekdays, rush hour traffic within Phoenix can be quite heavy. If you plan to visit Sedona on a weekday, you might consider staying on the northern end of Scottsdale for a convenient getaway. JW Marriott Phoenix Desert Ridge Resort & Spa and Fairmont Scottsdale Princess are good options.

Be aware that traffic within Uptown Sedona can be challenging, especially during peak times. The word is out, and the area gets crowded. Arriving in the town center as early as possible can help, but if you're visiting on a weekend or during Spring Break, for example, be prepared to be patient.

Finding parking can be difficult in popular areas. The Courthouse Vista parking lot offers the best access to Bell Rock, but try to arrive early or close to sunset to secure a spot. In town, parking can fill up quickly, and you may have to walk from one of the more distant lots. If someone in your group has mobility challenges, consider dropping them off before searching for parking, which can sometimes feel like it's in New Mexico. However, there are parking lots available, so don't lose heart—just follow the signs.

Don't forget to bring your America the Beautiful National Parks Pass! It is accepted at several locations in and around Sedona, granting you free admission or free parking.

If possible, choose a Sedona restaurant with a breathtaking view for lunch, unless you plan to have an early dinner or visit when sunset occurs late in the day. Once the sun sets in Sedona, it becomes pitch black.

If you can fit it into your schedule, consider booking a Sedona photo session. We had a fantastic experience doing this during our girls' trip to Sedona!

3 Options for a Sedona Day Trip from Phoenix

These three Sedona itineraries for a one-day trip provide options for morning, mid-day, and afternoon activities. I intentionally left out most dining suggestions because the area is compact, offering plenty of excellent choices that I'll outline in the next section.

Option 1: The Relaxing Sedona Day Trip
If you're seeking relaxation in Arizona, you're not alone. The Grand Canyon State is dotted with spas and golf courses at every turn. With this one-day Sedona itinerary, you'll experience Sedona's unique ambiance without any physically demanding activities.

Begin your day with a visit to the renowned Amitabha Stupa and Peace Park in Sedona. This serene space, located at the base of Thunder Mountain, is believed to radiate a sense of peace transcending religious boundaries.

While we took a scenic hike from our fantastic Sedona vacation rental to reach the Stupa, there is dedicated parking available for this popular site. Just remember to be respectful of the local residents, as the Stupa is located in a neighborhood. It's a wonderful place to enjoy the scenery and spend some quiet moments of reflection. The stupa and prayer flags provide a striking contrast against the backdrop of the red rocks.

Next, head to Tlaquepaque Arts & Crafts Village, conveniently located in town but away from the bustling Route 89A. The village has been a focal point of Sedona's thriving art scene since the 1970s. You'll find an abundance of galleries and boutiques beyond your imagination, and the complex's architecture will transport you to a Moroccan riad. Enjoy gallery hopping, savor a delightful lunch, grab a coffee, and immerse yourself in the overall ambiance.

Your final stop is just a short stroll away. Treat yourself to a decadent massage and detox in the steamy steam room at Los Abrigados Resort & Spa. Between you and me, it was one of the best massages I've ever had!

The hotel itself is beautiful and offers a great place to stay if you wish to extend your visit. Booking a massage grants you full-day access to the hotel's facilities, including the spacious fitness room and inviting outdoor pool.

Option 2: The Adventurous Day Trip to Sedona from Phoenix
Sedona provides an excellent playground for outdoor enthusiasts who crave fresh air, physical challenges, and adrenaline rushes. Be sure to bring plenty of water, as the elevation and low humidity can take a toll on your body.

Start your Sedona day trip with an early arrival at the Courthouse Vista parking lot. Snagging a coveted parking spot will allow you to explore the lower and upper Bell Rock trails, ultimately reaching the summit. [Info about hike distance/time and summit]. The views from the top are breathtaking, and you'll appreciate their splendor even more knowing you've conquered the challenge.

After a well-deserved lunch at Mesa Grill at the Sedona airport, make your way into town to check in for an off-road Jeep tour. Accompanied by an experienced guide, you'll embark on an unforgettable off-roading adventure in a specially equipped Jeep. For adrenaline junkies, I highly recommend the Diamondback Gulch tour. It offers non-stop boulder crawling, exhilaratingly steep descents and ascents, and breathtaking views that stretch for miles and miles.

Whichever member of your group tends to experience motion sickness the most should definitely take the front seat during the Pink Jeep Tours. Also, avoid wearing a white shirt, as I did, as it will likely become stained with dirt during the tour. It's advisable to bring a light jacket or fleece for the ride back in the evening, as it can get chilly.

I must provide a word of caution regarding Pink Jeep Tours with kids. While their website mentions the availability of car seats, as a car seat technician,

I felt uneasy once we arrived. The Jeeps are equipped with lap belts and have ample padding around the roll cage. Although you can install a harnessed car seat on the back bench, there is no top tether available, so it is best suited for rear-facing children. Car seats are not tested for use in side-facing seats, and booster seats are not approved for use with lap belts. The route to the National Forest includes travel on major paved roads before reaching more remote areas.

Upon returning to town, take the opportunity to explore and window shop at the local galleries. Sedona is home to a diverse community of artists, each showcasing their own interpretation of the local culture and natural beauty.

Option 3: A Historical Journey through Sedona
While the majority of Arizona's population resides in the southern and central parts of the state, the most intriguing history can be found further north. This Sedona day trip itinerary diverges from the previous two as the first two stops are not in Sedona itself. Nevertheless, they are well worth your time.

Head west from your route along I-17 and step back into the "wild west" in the old mining town of Jerome. Established in the 1880s for copper mining, it reached its peak in the 1920s thanks to the efforts of the United Verde Extension Mining Company. Over time, much of Jerome suffered from fires and collapses, leading to multiple reconstructions, until eventually many residents left to seek fortunes elsewhere.

To learn about Jerome's fascinating history and see important relics, begin your visit at Jerome State Historic Park. Don't miss the informative movie, which provides valuable context for what you'll encounter in the town. After exploring the museum, venture into the remaining town to discover remnants of historic buildings intertwined with newer shops, some of which embrace Jerome's new identity as a haven for hippies. In town, you'll also find the small Jerome Mine Museum, which focuses on the town and its inhabitants. For a more enriching experience, consider taking a guided tour to bring the town to life as you stroll through its streets.

I recommend having lunch in Jerome, as there will be some time before you reach Sedona proper. Haunted Hamburger, conveniently located in the heart of town, comes highly recommended.

Back on the highway, your next stop takes you further back into Arizona's history. Montezuma's Castle is a remarkably preserved Sinagua cliff dwelling dating back to around 1100-1400. A self-guided visit to this National Monument takes approximately 30-45 minutes along a fully accessible path. I recommend watching the park movie for a deeper understanding of the site. Admission is free with the America the Beautiful National Parks Pass.

During my most recent visit, I encountered a group of rangers discussing the evolving interpretation of the site's story. Advancements in scientific methods and increased involvement of local tribes in collecting oral histories have contributed to a greater understanding of the site beyond traditional archaeological digs.

Finally, you'll make your way to Sedona, where you'll be astounded by the breathtaking scenery of the red rocks. Head directly to Pink Jeep Tours in Uptown for the Ancient Ruins tour, which takes you deep into the Coconino National Forest to the Honanki Heritage Site.

While Montezuma's Castle provides an impressive example high on the cliff face, Honanki is located at a lower elevation, offering a unique opportunity to observe intricate details. You'll witness the evolution of the Sinagua's construction methods over time as they adopted techniques from other Native American communities. The site also features thousands of pictograms that provide insights into different eras of its use.

Honanki holds great significance for the local Hopi community and continues to be used for rituals today. As a result, the tour schedule may have some gaps, so check ahead for your planned visit date. Note that there is approximately 15 minutes of walking each way, including sections on uneven forest paths.

Your visit to Honanki will coincide with the setting sun, casting a stunning glow on the surrounding red rocks. It's the perfect way to end your day in Sedona! Your driver will return you to town, where you're free to explore the art galleries and enjoy dinner at one of the many restaurants listed below.

Where to Stay in Sedona
After reading about all the amazing things to do in Sedona, you may decide it's worth staying for a few nights. When choosing where to stay in Sedona, consider the activities you plan to prioritize. If you'll be spending most of your time in town, such as taking Sedona Jeep tours and visiting art galleries, it's advisable to stay in Uptown Sedona, within walking distance of the heart of town to avoid traffic at peak times. If your focus is on hiking or visiting historic sites outside of town, staying outside the town center may provide a more tranquil experience.

Best Western Plus Arroyo Roble Hotel & Creekside Villas – A top choice for families, offering free breakfast, a pool, a game room, stunning views, and a central location in Uptown.

Hyatt Residence Club Sedona Piñon Pointe – A great option for avoiding traffic and parking without being right in Uptown. It is also conveniently located close to excellent dining options.

Los Abrigados Resort & Spa – Ideal for art lovers, as it is located at the Tlaquepaque Arts & Crafts Village.

L'Auberge de Sedona – The epitome of luxury in Sedona, albeit with a higher price tag.

Sedona Vacation Rental – For groups and families, this lovely Airbnb is situated in a peaceful residential area near the Stupa.

Where to Eat in Sedona
Sedona offers two types of restaurants: those with breathtaking views and those without. After many years of visiting, I can confidently say that choosing a Sedona restaurant with the best view for lunch is preferable, unless you're dining during a late sunset. The good news is that you'll find excellent restaurants in Sedona across various price ranges.

Tamaliza Cafe is a budget-friendly restaurant with a view. They serve excellent, authentic Mexican food prepared from scratch in their small kitchen. Try to secure a seat at the bar facing the front window for great views while you dine.

Wildflower is known for its outstanding soups, salads, and sandwiches. Enjoy your meal on their scenic patio or in the airy dining room.

Pisa Lisa is the place to go for fantastic gourmet pizzas, which can be enjoyed on-site or taken to go. Keep in mind that there may be a long wait, so consider calling ahead with your order.

Fiesta Mexican serves up delicious and affordable Mexican food. While it doesn't offer a view due to its orientation, it's a suitable choice for dining at the end of a busy day.

Mesa Grill is one of Sedona's most renowned restaurants, thanks to its view and proximity to "the Vortex." However, securing a reservation can be incredibly difficult, so I recommend calling well in advance, particularly

if you plan to dine here for lunch or an hour before sunset.

The Vault is a nice restaurant conveniently located with great views. They offer patio dining, making it a good option for a fancy lunch with Option 1 or Option 2 Sedona itineraries. Make sure to reserve early. While we enjoyed a pleasant dinner there, unfortunately, it was too dark to fully appreciate the spectacular view.

Rascal Modern Diner serves delightful food and is owned by the same group as Mesa Grill. While it doesn't offer a view, the fresh and tasty dishes make up for it.

Chapter 21: Your Arizona Packing List

Other than the places where I have lived, I have spent more time in Arizona than any other location. Over the past 25 years, I have visited the state dozens of times, ranging from short weekend trips to extended stays as I explored every corner of Arizona.

This packing list for an Arizona vacation is a compilation of my knowledge and experience gained from my extensive time in the Grand Canyon State. While some items may seem obvious, there are a few things that I have occasionally forgotten and deeply regretted. This packing list includes not only what to wear in Arizona but also items that you may not have considered but are essential for your trip.

America the Beautiful National Parks Pass

Arizona is home to numerous incredible national parks, monuments, historic sites, and more. If you plan to visit even a few of these destinations (or venture into neighboring Southwest states on a longer road trip), the America the Beautiful National Parks Pass offers exceptional value for your money.

How does the pass work? You can purchase it in advance here and activate it at the first site you visit. While some smaller sites may not punch the date, you can simply display the pass in your windshield or hang it from your mirror to enjoy the extra time. The pass remains valid until the end of the 12th month after activation.

With the pass, you'll have unlimited admission to all National Park Service properties in the United States. For just $80, you can gain fee-free admission for your vehicle to the following Arizona sites:

- Grand Canyon National Park ($35)
- Petrified Forest National Park ($25)
- Saguaro National Park ($25)
- Sedona Red Rocks ($5 daily/$15 weekly)

- Montezuma Castle & Tuzigoot National Monuments ($10 per adult; pass covers up to 4 adults)
- Organ Pipe Cactus National Monument ($25)
- Tonto National Monument ($10)
- Sunset Crater & Wupatki National Monuments ($25)
- Walnut Canyon National Monument ($25)

As you can see, the America the Beautiful Pass is an excellent addition to your Arizona road trip packing list. You can even use it to visit Sedona Red Rocks, including popular trails like Cathedral Rock and Bell Rock.

Heavy-duty water filter bottle
I have a confession to make, Arizona: Your water quality is not the best. I'm not afraid to say it, and I know many others feel the same way.

Water in Arizona, particularly in the central and southern parts of the state, is notoriously hard due to high calcium and magnesium concentrations. While it is not necessarily harmful to health, it poses challenges when it comes to getting things and people clean because it prevents soaps and detergents from lathering effectively.

In many areas, the solution to this issue is installing a water softening system. However, this results in water that tastes unpleasant, especially for those sensitive to unfamiliar water like myself.

During my recent trip to Arizona, I found a great solution: the GRAYL. This heavy-duty purifying bottle worked wonders and also served me well during my trip to Mexico. The GRAYL features a three-stage filter, including an electrostatic mesh, which eliminates bacteria, heavy metals, and even viruses. With the GRAYL, you can enjoy clean and safe drinking water wherever you are in Arizona, and it tastes better too.

If you're traveling solo, the GRAYL Geopress with a capacity of 24 oz and a filtration time of less than a minute may be sufficient. I recommend filling the bottle slightly below the "max" line to minimize spilling during the filtration process. If you're on a budget, you might find the lower-priced Ultralight version suitable, although it lacks a dedicated drinking top (though it doesn't pose a problem for us).

For those who require greater capacity or prefer super-cold water, consider pairing the GRAYL with a high-capacity Camelbak or insulated water bottles. The insulated bottles are sized for convenience, fitting comfortably in your hands and cup holders while effectively keeping your drink cool.

I personally filter a full load in the GRAYL, refrigerate it for an hour or two, transfer it to my insulated bottles, and then refill the GRAYL. It may sound complicated, but it worked perfectly for me.

If the GRAYL is beyond your budget, you may consider Hydaway bottles with charcoal filters. We used these on a previous trip to Tucson and Saguaro National Park, and they did a good job of filtering out some of the taste. Additionally, they pack down easily for travel.

While I generally dislike single-use plastics, I make exceptions when it comes to safety in the desert. For a lengthy Arizona road trip where you may find yourself far from civilization for hours at a time, it's advisable to keep one or two gallon jugs from the grocery store in your trunk, just in case. While driving between Tucson, Phoenix, Sedona, and Flagstaff won't require it, venturing further east or west may necessitate having extra water on hand.

Two pairs of shoes for Arizona
The footwear you pack for your Arizona trip will largely depend on your planned activities. In general, I recommend bringing two pairs of shoes. The specific options will vary based on your planned activities.

For an Arizona road trip that combines outdoor adventures with city exploration, you'll want a sturdy pair of sneakers or hiking shoes and a pair of casual shoes. In November through February, closed shoes are preferable, while sandals or flip flops are suitable from March through October. Keep in mind that certain activities, such as horseback riding and some tours, may require closed shoes.

I managed all of our "light hiking" during our recent trip with a pair of sneakers with added inserts for support. These sneakers also worked well for casual time in Scottsdale. For moderate to serious hiking, I prefer trail runners for their breathability and support. It's important to note that any shoes worn while hiking will likely get dusty, especially in the northern regions where the red dirt tends to linger. You might even consider bringing a shoe-cleaning kit to maintain the appearance of your nicer shoes.

If you plan on engaging in serious hiking, including exploring the Grand Canyon, it's essential to have appropriate hiking boots on your Arizona packing list.

During the warmer months, it can be convenient to have a pair of nice-looking sandals for strolling around town and a durable pair of comfortable flip flops for poolside relaxation.

Sun protection - for your entire body
It comes as no surprise that the sun in Arizona is strong and requires adequate protection. Even in March, we experienced sunburns despite wearing sunscreen (although it wasn't my preferred brand, but a cheaper alternative I purchased upon arrival).

While it may not be practical to cover your entire body at all times, it's important to have options that allow you to protect yourself when necessary. Sunscreen is an obvious defense and works effectively. I highly recommend this mineral-based cream, which not only offers great protection but also smells pleasant (although it's not the one we used during our recent encounter with UV rays).

Lip balm serves two purposes: protecting your lips from painful sunburns and preventing dryness in the arid climate of Arizona.

In hindsight, I wish I had brought a lightweight, long-sleeved shirt with me on my trip. There were times when I experienced discomfort due to a peculiar condition, and having more coverage would have saved me from that. It's also more convenient than constantly reapplying sunscreen during long hikes and other activities.

If you don't mind wearing hats, they are an excellent way to shield your face and eyes from the harsh rays of the sun. Opting for a wide-brim hat can also provide protection for your neck.

Sunglasses are essential for both comfort and the long-term health of your eyes. Studies have shown that excessive sun exposure can lead to vision damage.

For those planning to spend time in outdoor pools, which is a common activity in Arizona, a rash guard not only keeps your skin safe but also reduces the need for sunscreen (which can be inconvenient and costly). I highly recommend this versatile option, which can also be used as a long-sleeved shirt when needed.

Daypack for activities
Regardless of the type of trip you're planning, it's important to have a reliable daypack on your Arizona packing list. At the very least, you'll need it to carry water. Additionally, it comes in handy for storing your camera, snacks, sunscreen, and other essentials.

My personal favorite is the Tortuga Setout packable backpack (unfortunately, it has been discontinued), but the Eddie Bauer pack is a nearly identical alternative. These packs are lightweight, pack down small, and provide some structure when expanded. They feature a mesh back panel and straps for enhanced comfort and include two water bottle sleeves. This is an excellent choice for a mix of light hiking and urban exploration.

For a more substantial daypack suitable for urban adventures, we use the WAYB Ready to Roam backpack with the attached Catchall. It has proven to be durable, high-capacity, well-organized, and aesthetically pleasing. It even accommodates a Camelbak bladder in the laptop sleeve.

If your Arizona trip is focused on outdoor activities, consider investing in a proper hiking daypack. Explore different options to find the one that best fits your needs and budget.

Swimwear
Whether you're relaxing by a beautiful resort pool in Scottsdale, soothing your muscles in a hot tub after a day of hiking, or enjoying Arizona's natural water sources, a swimsuit is a must-have item on your packing list.

Personally, I recommend bringing two swimsuits to Arizona. If you have a place to hang one outside (inside out to prevent fading), it should dry quickly. However, having a backup suit is useful in case the timing doesn't work out. Swimsuits take up minimal space, and some can serve dual purposes, such as trunks that can double as shorts or supportive swim tops for women that work as sports bras.

Reusable snack containers
If you aspire to be an environmentally responsible traveler, consider including reusable snack containers on your Arizona packing list. Having food with you can be beneficial, especially when venturing outside major cities.

A simple option is a basic reusable snack bag, which comes in various styles. These washable, food-safe bags keep your treats, whether wet or dry, separate from everything else. They are lightweight, collapsible, and easy to clean. They are particularly useful for full-day hikes or long drives when you want to bring your lunch.

Light jacket
While it may not immediately come to mind, having a jacket is important for your Arizona trip. Once the sun sets, the bone-dry air cools considerably, except during the hottest summer months. Even in Phoenix and Tucson, a jacket is necessary from October through March.

Fleece jackets are practical for most seasons, but any style will suffice. Personally, I enjoy wearing this new fleece jacket for its classy appearance. In winter, a proper jacket is recommended, although packable puffer jackets have served us well.

For winter trips to northern Arizona, layering is crucial. Consider wearing thermal sets under your clothes, adding a cozy mid-layer like the fleece mentioned above, and topping it off with a puffer jacket. This combination keeps you warm while allowing flexibility to remove layers as your body heats up during hikes.

A rain jacket is typically not necessary for Arizona trips, but if you're planning outdoor activities from July to September, consider packing a packable rain jacket. The monsoon season brings afternoon rain showers, and it's important to seek shelter in case of heavy downpours to avoid flash flooding and lightning risks.

Cell phone charging cable
Your cell phone will likely be your go-to device for navigation, music, photos, and more during your Arizona trip. Be sure to bring a charging cable to plug it into your car to avoid being stranded in remote areas without navigation.

For added preparedness, consider bringing a portable charger as well.

Map and/or Arizona guidebook

While most parts of the state have reliable cell phone service, there are areas with limited connectivity, particularly when driving on back roads or taking scenic detours. Including a durable and compact state map in your packing list can be helpful if you find yourself venturing further afield. It's less cumbersome than the oversized AAA AZ map we used in the past.

Even if you stick to main roads, having a guidebook can enhance your trip by providing history, context, and unexpected gems along the way. It also keeps everyone engaged in the car, as one person can narrate the journey.

Chapter 22: Best Scottsdale Resorts For Families

If you're planning a family trip to Scottsdale and wondering where to stay, consider these excellent resorts that families adore. They are praised for their convenient locations and amenities designed with kids in mind. Whether you're on a budget or seeking luxury, there's a perfect family-friendly option in Scottsdale to suit your needs.

Top Resorts in Scottsdale for Families

While many resorts in Scottsdale cater to families, a few stand out for their exceptional features. Here are my recommendations for the best family-friendly places to stay in Scottsdale.

Hyatt Regency Gainey Ranch

Officially known as the Hyatt Regency Scottsdale Resort & Spa At Gainey Ranch, this resort is on my personal list of must-visit places! Let me tell you why it's so incredible.

Firstly, the property is simply stunning. I've driven by it numerous times, admiring the beautiful grounds. The pool area is absolutely amazing, featuring water slides, a sandy beach, and a 2.5-acre "water playground." Additionally, there are fantastic amenities for older kids and adults, such as a spa, rock climbing wall, tennis courts, a putting green, and family games like giant Jenga and chess.

Beyond the facilities, the Hyatt Regency Scottsdale offers an array of activities for the whole family to enjoy, making it one of the most family-friendly resorts in Scottsdale. Highlights include guided nature walks, poolside games, and Native American crafts. Every Friday afternoon, there's a 4pm presentation on Arizona birds of prey, followed by a 4:30pm Native American dance performance. The resort also hosts live music performances on weekends.

If you're seeking a relaxing family vacation in Scottsdale where you can simply unwind and enjoy the resort's offerings, this is the perfect choice for you!

A note for 2023: This Scottsdale family resort is currently undergoing renovations to become a Grand Hyatt. Although some favorite features like the kid-focused Camp Hyatt may not be available during this time, it will undoubtedly become one of the best kid-friendly hotels in Scottsdale once the renovations are complete.

Fairmont Princess Scottsdale
For luxurious family resorts in Scottsdale, look no further than the Fairmont Princess Scottsdale. It's so incredible that even local families opt for a staycation there!

Think of the Fairmont as an all-inclusive resort in Cancun (excluding the cost of food). It offers golf, six pools (including water slides and a toddler-friendly zero-entry option), an amazing spa, a beach, and fun seasonal activities like ice skating in the desert. There's even a kids club (ages 5-12) and a recreation center with activities for the whole family! You'll never be bored, even if you never leave the resort.

The rooms at the Fairmont are generously sized, with over 500 square feet of space. While the location is quite far north, it's perfect for family-friendly hiking in the McDowell Sonoran Preserve, shopping and dining at Kierland Commons, or exploring the Musical Instrument Museum—a unique experience for kids in Scottsdale.

Additionally, the Fairmont offers a guests-only car rental desk, making it easy to borrow a car and explore the surrounding area during your stay!

Westin Kierland Resort & Spa
The Westin Kierland Resort & Spa is a fan favorite and well-known as one of the best family hotels in Scottsdale. It's particularly ideal for families with children who love water activities. The Adventure Water Park boasts pools, a lazy river, a massive waterslide, and even a FlowRider wave simulator for surfing enthusiasts.

For those seeking non-water-based activities, the resort offers a luxurious spa, a golf course, and numerous highly-regarded restaurants. There's also a kids club and the option to make s'mores over the fire pit on weekends. Guests can relax with lawn games or attend the Friday reptile presentation in the lobby.

When you're ready to venture beyond the resort, you'll find yourself just steps away from Kierland Commons and Scottsdale Quarter, which offer shopping, dining, and lifestyle experiences. Additionally, you have the option to rent a car on-site if you only need one for a few days or plan to take a day trip to Sedona, for example.

DoubleTree by Hilton Paradise Valley Resort Scottsdale
If you're seeking a budget-friendly hotel in Scottsdale for families, the DoubleTree in Paradise Valley (located within an independent town

surrounded by Scottsdale) is an excellent choice. It enjoys an incredibly convenient location, just a mile from Fashion Square and Old Town Scottsdale. This proximity also puts it closer to many favorite Phoenix attractions, including the Desert Botanical Garden and the zoo.

The DoubleTree features two pools with ample seating, as well as a lovely outdoor dining area. There's also a spacious gym, a putting green, and tennis courts.

In a heartwarming departure from most other resorts, the DoubleTree in Scottsdale provides free parking for their guests—a refreshing surprise! This is especially noteworthy if you're planning a week-long stay in Scottsdale during spring break, as parking fees can add up significantly.

For families looking for a balance of pool time and exploring the exciting family activities in Scottsdale and Phoenix, the DoubleTree Resort in Scottsdale offers great value and an ideal balance. It's considered one of the top kid-friendly resorts in Scottsdale AZ, providing families with an excellent vacation experience while stretching their vacation dollars!

Chapter 23: 10 Most Famous Foods in Arizona

Arizona is renowned for its diverse cuisine, influenced by the abundance of the desert, Native American traditions, and its proximity to Mexico. With its unique climate, geographical location, and rich cultural heritage, the state offers a variety of iconic dishes that are sure to satisfy anyone seeking novelty and flavor in their next meal.

Chimichangas

Originating in Tucson, AZ, the famous chimichanga is a large, deep-fried burrito often served with sour cream, guacamole, rice, and beans. According to legend, it was created when Monica Flin, the founder of El Charro Café, accidentally dropped a bean burrito into hot oil. This happy accident led to the birth of the chimichanga.

Chimichangas can be found in countless Mexican restaurants throughout Arizona. Notable places to try this iconic dish include Valle Luna Mexican Restaurant and Rito's Mexican Food in Phoenix, as well as the legendary El Charro Café.

Fry Bread/Navajo Tacos

Fry bread originated out of necessity when the Navajo Tribe was forced to leave their land and travel to New Mexico. They were provided with flour, water, salt, and lard, which became the ingredients for this iconic dish.

Fry bread has gained such popularity that you can embark on a pre-mapped 346-mile fry bread road trip, spanning from Casa Blanca in southern Arizona to Kayenta in the north, with eight delicious stops along the way.

This Native American dish can be enjoyed in three main ways: as Navajo Tacos topped with meat, beans, cheese, and lettuce; as a crepe-style treat with honey, cinnamon, or powdered sugar; or simply plain or with beans and cheese.

Prickly Pear Cactus/Nopales

The prickly pear cactus offers edible fruits known as prickly pears, which have a flavor resembling a blend of watermelon and bubblegum. Throughout Arizona, you'll find prickly pears incorporated into various forms, including jellies, candies, juices, sodas, sauces, margaritas, and even coffee and popcorn.

The green pads of the prickly pear cactus, called nopales, are also edible and widely used in Mexican cuisine. They can be found in dishes such as nopales tacos, quesadillas, con pollo (with chicken), and sandwiches. Prepared nopales have a texture similar to French beans, asparagus, or okra, and can be enjoyed raw, sautéed, or steamed.

Sonoran Hot Dogs

A beloved delicacy in Arizona, the Sonoran Hot Dog—also known as SHD—is a grilled, bacon-wrapped hot dog served on a bolillo-style bun. It's typically topped with beans, mustard, mayo, onions, tomatoes, and green salsa. While the style originated in Hermosillo, Mexico, it has become a staple in southern Arizona cuisine.

When searching for an authentic Sonoran Hot Dog, it's best to seek recommendations from locals. There has been recent controversy surrounding the popular vendors, locally known as "dogueros," among those less experienced in the world of SHDs. The popularity of Sonoran Hot Dogs in Arizona has grown over the past 20 years, even though they gained prominence in Sonora, Mexico, only in the 1980s.

Mother Road Brewing

Though not technically considered food, the Tower Station IPA from Mother Road Brewing Company in Flagstaff is highly regarded and can be considered a form of sustenance. The brewery takes its name from John Steinbeck's designation of Route 66 as "the mother road" in his novel Grapes of Wrath. Tower Station IPA, named after a historic gas station in Shamrock, TX, features a copper-orange hue, tangerine and pineapple aromas, Pilsner and Pale malts, and flavors of grapefruit peel and pine. With a 93/100 rating on a reputable beer connoisseur website, it is often hailed as the most esteemed IPA in Arizona.

Mother Road Brewing is also committed to environmental conservation. They employ a carbon recapture system, which captures and reinjects carbon released during the brewing process back into their beers. Additionally, a portion of the proceeds from a specific beer is donated to protect native species in the state.

Salsa

Arizona is known for its exceptional Mexican food, and it's no surprise that a pre-mapped Salsa Trail exists in Southeast Arizona. This trail takes you to 11 to 13 renowned Mexican restaurants in Graham, Greenlee, and Cochise counties, with the headquarters located in Safford. When embarking on this saucy adventure, inform the host at your first stop that you're participating in the Salsa Trail, and you'll receive a "salsa passport" to track your flavorful journey.

Cheese Crisps

The Arizona cheese crisp is akin to a quesadilla without the tortilla on top. It is believed to have originated as a solution to the problem of day-old tortillas losing their freshness. To counter this, someone came up with the idea of crisping the tortillas to hasten the inevitable stiffening process.

Popular in restaurants across the state, cheese crisps are made by crisping thin, butter-covered flour tortillas on a pizza pan. Once the tortilla reaches the desired level of crispiness, cheese is sprinkled on top, and it's returned to the oven just long enough to melt the cheese. Often, sliced green chiles garnish the dish, arranged in a star pattern on the cheese before it goes back in the oven.

Medjool Dates

Yuma, known as the "Sunniest City on Earth," and the nearby Bard Valley are the largest producers of premium-quality Medjool dates globally. Medjool dates were brought to the United States from Morocco to save the trees from a disease outbreak.

In Yuma and the surrounding region, date farms offer tours and a range of date-based products, including date milkshakes, date coleslaw, and date bread. The area is proud of its date palm trees, with some standing over 70 feet tall since their arrival in 1930.

Rock Springs Pies

When it comes to iconic foods in Arizona, Rock Springs Café is a game-changer. Despite not being the first thing that comes to mind, their pies have garnered rave reviews like "out of this world" and "I could eat the Jack Daniel's pecan pie a la mode every day of my life." This small café, located in the unincorporated town of Black Canyon City north of Phoenix, has become a must-visit destination for food enthusiasts, earning the title of

"The Pie Capital of Arizona" in the Phoenix New Times. While their Jack Daniels Pecan Pie is their signature dish, the display case showcases a wide array of pies, including apple crumb, pumpkin, and chocolate cream.

Piki

While not a commonly found dish in the southwestern desert, Piki holds significant cultural value. It is a thin, papery, unleavened "bread" with sacred origins, traditionally reserved for special ceremonies among the Hopi tribe of Arizona.

The piki stone, a cherished possession, is heated and then seasoned with oils from seeds and animal fats. The batter is swiftly smeared onto the hot, preheated piki stone and immediately peeled off, creating an exceptionally thin sheet of "bread." The preparation of piki is a day-long process carried out by women in a dedicated piki house.

If you find yourself passing through Arizona, make sure to stop by for their famous chimichangas. What better opportunity to indulge in a deep-fried burrito than in the place where it originated? However, if you have the luxury of time during your Arizona adventure, the Southwest has much more to offer—diverse cuisine, stunning desert landscapes, and unique plant life thriving in the warm climate.

Chapter 24: Flagstaff Gateway to Adventure

Explore the vibrant city of Flagstaff, a destination in its own right near the Grand Canyon National Park. Flagstaff offers a plethora of all-season recreational activities, opportunities to immerse in nature, bustling dining and shopping scenes, a revitalized historic downtown area, a renowned observatory, and three nearby national monuments.

Founded in 1876 and named after a majestic ponderosa pine flagpole erected to commemorate the nation's centennial, Flagstaff has long been a hub for transportation, economy, and outdoor recreation in northern Arizona. Embracing its pioneering history, the city still preserves remnants of its past. The revitalized Heritage Square remains the heart of Flagstaff, while historic establishments like the Hotel Monte Vista, Weatherford Hotel, and Babbett Brothers outfitters stand as testaments to the city's mining and railroad roots. Historic storefronts now house galleries, boutiques, coffee shops, restaurants, museums, and various businesses.

Despite its urbanized areas with shopping centers and residential communities, Flagstaff has managed to retain its soul. Look no further than the towering San Francisco Peaks, revered by the local indigenous cultures, to understand the city's strong connection to nature and outdoor activities.

During the busy summer season when accommodations near the Grand Canyon and Tusayan are fully booked, Flagstaff offers a range of options, including national motel chains and charming B&Bs like the renovated Victorian England House. Whether you visit for a specific reason or simply to explore the dynamic town, you'll find plenty of reasons to extend your stay and discover Flagstaff's charms. Don't miss the exciting day trips available in the surrounding area.

If you have just a day to spare in Flagstaff, you can choose to focus on history, nature, or shopping. Nature enthusiasts can begin their day at the Flagstaff Arboretum, a sprawling 200-acre space of natural and landscaped woodlands. Take a leisurely stroll along shaded paths, join a birdwatching walk or a program focused on hawks and raptors, explore the demonstration gardens, or embark on a nature trail hike while learning about the diverse wildflowers, shrubs, and trees of northern Arizona.

For a quick pick-me-up, indulge in a cup of coffee from popular spots like Wicked Arizona Coffee, Late for the Train Coffee, or enjoy a more substantial meal at Macy's European Coffeehouse, Bakery & Vegetarian Restaurant. If you're in the mood for a snack, head to the Flagstaff Chocolate Company or the Sweet Shoppe and Nut House, both located in Old Town Shops at Heritage Square.

When it's time for lunch, transport yourself back in time at the classic Route 66-style Galaxy Diner, or savor all-American flavors at Fratelli Pizza, Beaver Street Brewpub, or Downtown Diner, followed by a homemade pie or an ice cream sundae. If you're craving Asian cuisine, Swaddee Authentic Thai Cuisine or Karma Sushi Bar & Grill are excellent options.

Continue your adventures with an otherworldly experience at Lowell Observatory, a renowned center for celestial observations since 1894. This historic site, where Pluto was discovered in 1930, has been recognized by Time Magazine as one of "The World's 100 Most Important Places." Enjoy daily tours of the telescopes, engage in daytime solar viewing, or indulge in an evening of stargazing.

Northern Arizona's history is steeped in mining, railroads, and Native American heritage. The Museum of Northern Arizona showcases modern and traditional Indian arts, artifacts, and natural science, providing insights into the region's rich cultural tapestry. A visit to the Arizona Pioneer Museum, housed in the 1908 Hospital for the Indigent and featuring a steam locomotive at its entrance, offers a glimpse into life from the Territorial period to the heyday of Route 66. To experience the lifestyle of lumber barons in 1904, explore Riordan Mansion State Park, a magnificent

40-room log mansion built by the Riordan brothers, who married sisters and designed the mansion with identical wings and communal living spaces.

For those in the mood for shopping, downtown Flagstaff offers a delightful array of options. Browse through shops specializing in turquoise jewelry, Navajo rugs, and museum-quality Indian pottery, or refresh your western wardrobe. Begin your shopping excursion at Heritage Square and explore the eclectic stores and eateries at the Old Town Shops complex. Then, wander along the sidewalks, discovering boutiques, outdoor outfitters, bookstores, art galleries, and numerous places to enjoy snacks, drinks, or meals. The dining choices range from American, Mexican, Thai, and Japanese to vegetarian restaurants, diners, sandwich shops, coffee houses, and microbreweries.

As the day comes to an end, make reservations for an evening of fine dining and entertainment at Josephine's American Bistro, a beloved restaurant in Flagstaff. Alternatively, catch a lively music review at Black Barts Steakhouse, a family-friendly establishment offering a wide range of entrees. If you're up for more excitement, visit the Museum Club, a historic Route 66 roadhouse dating back to 1931. Enjoy some boot-scootin', beer-chugging, live music, and perhaps even encounter the ghostly legend of a murdered patron.

Chapter 25: Top Things to Do in Flagstaff

There are plenty of activities to enjoy in Flagstaff, as well as some amazing experiences just outside the city, such as a visit to the Grand Canyon National Park. Depending on your preferences, the season, and the amount of time you have, there are numerous fantastic things to do and explore. Let's start with a quick summary of the top five essential activities in Flagstaff before delving into the other wonderful possibilities. All of these options are family-friendly, and most even welcome dogs.

1. Explore Downtown Flagstaff: Start your day with a cup of coffee at Macy's, Rendezvous, or Late for the Train. Enjoy a refreshing beer at one of the many microbreweries, indulge in delicious food at local eateries, listen to live music on the streets or in establishments, and join in the vibrant festivities happening in Heritage Square.

2. Drive up Snowbowl Road: If you're visiting during summer, take a scenic chair lift ride at Arizona Snowbowl or embark on a short hike from Aspen Corner. In the fall, relish in the breathtaking sights of the changing aspen leaves. During winter, consider skiing or snowboarding at Snowbowl. Regardless of the season, the beauty of Snowbowl Road will captivate you.

3. Visit Lowell Observatory: A must-visit attraction, Lowell Observatory is famous for its discovery of Pluto. The observatory recently opened a new observation deck in the summer of 2019, adding to the already incredible experience of observing the night sky through their telescopes. Attend workshops, informative talks, and explore fascinating exhibits that offer an up-close and personal encounter with space.

4. Explore the Museum of Northern Arizona: Flagstaff holds a deep connection to Native American culture, and the Museum of Northern Arizona beautifully showcases this heritage. The museum offers educational and historical exhibits, often sparking discussions about preserving and honoring Native American traditions in our modern society.

5. Take a Stroll at Buffalo Park: Set aside some time to walk the loop at Buffalo Park, a serene and picturesque location that truly represents the essence of Flagstaff. You'll often spot deer leisurely roaming while people enjoy walking or running with their dogs. Enjoy breathtaking views of the San Francisco Peaks and Mount Elden, and embrace the opportunity for a peaceful exercise in the midst of nature.

These top five activities provide a taste of what Flagstaff has to offer, ensuring an enjoyable and enriching experience during your visit.

Chapter 26: Top Things To See & Do On Route 66

These remarkable Route 66 offers an abundance of attractions, including iconic landmarks, charming roadside diners, retro neon signs, world-renowned museums, and spectacular national parks. Known as the "Mother Road," it holds a significant place in American culture, traversing the heart of the country and providing insights into the individualism and idiosyncrasies of American society and culture. To experience authentic Americana, here are our recommended highlights of the key places to visit along Route 66.

1. Cadillac Ranch (Amarillo, Texas): A short 15-minute drive from Amarillo, Cadillac Ranch is a renowned site on Route 66. This public art installation and sculpture feature ten half-buried Cadillacs, adorned with graffiti, emerging from the Texan desert. Visitors are encouraged to contribute their own artwork by spray painting a section of their chosen Cadillac.

2. The Painted Desert (Indian Wells, Arizona): The vibrant colors and layered beauty of the Painted Desert are captivating. Located in northern Arizona's rocky badlands, this region showcases rocks in a kaleidoscope of hues, from sunrise pinks and oranges to deep greys and lavenders. Taking a detour from Route 66 allows you to witness the quintessential experience of watching the sunset over the Painted Desert, transforming the sky and rocks into a canvas of fiery colors.

3. The Milk Bottle Grocery (Oklahoma City, Oklahoma): A classic landmark along the Mother Road, the Milk Bottle Grocery in Oklahoma City features a giant milk bottle atop a traditional red brick building. Once a grocery and milk store, it now houses a Vietnamese café, serving bánh mì sandwiches and iced coffee—a unique blend of history and culinary delight.

4. St. Louis and the Gateway Arch (St. Louis, Missouri): As the first or second stop after starting the Route 66 drive from Chicago, St. Louis offers a fusion of culture, history, music, and sports. Situated along the Mississippi River, this city is known for its St. Louis Cardinals baseball team, beautiful Forest Park, and a remarkable culinary scene. The iconic Gateway Arch, a symbol of the city, provides sensational views of St. Louis from its 630-foot height.

5. Route 66 Hall of Fame Museum (Pontiac, Illinois): Standing one hundred miles from the traditional start point of Route 66, the Route 66 Hall of Fame Museum showcases thousands of historic memorabilia and artifacts from the heyday of the Mother Road. Capture a photo of the iconic Route 66 mural, delve into the road's history through images, and gain insights into the era when this route was America's most significant highway.

6. Ed Galloway's Totem Pole Park (Foyil, Oklahoma): Three miles off Route 66 lies Ed Galloway's Totem Pole Park, home to the world's largest concrete totem pole. Created by retired art teacher Ed Galloway in 1937, this park stands as Oklahoma's oldest and largest example of folk art. The expertly carved and painted structures mainly depict figurative images of

birds and Native Americans, offering a captivating display of artistic heritage.

7. Petrified Forest (Holbrook, Arizona): Before reaching Holbrook, a stop at the otherworldly Petrified Forest National Park is a must. This park houses the world's largest collection of petrified wood, some dating back 225 million years. Alongside vividly colored landscapes, visitors can explore the region's badlands wildlife and experience a strong Native American presence with ruins and petroglyphs.

8. Santa Monica Pier (Los Angeles, California): Marking the end point of Route 66, Santa Monica Pier is adorned with the iconic "Route 66 – End of the Trail" sign. This classic American sight features a big wheel against a picturesque sandy beach and the Pacific Ocean. The pier offers a historic carousel, an amusement park, free historical walking tours, and a range of dining options, making it a perfect spot for relaxation and entertainment.

9. The Blue Whale (Catoosa, Oklahoma): The Blue Whale of Catoosa stands as one of Route 66's most recognizable icons. Situated in a beautiful pond and surrounded by a shaded picnic area, it provides a delightful spot to pause and enjoy a meal before continuing the journey to Oklahoma City.

10. The Wigwam Motel (Holbrook, Arizona): One of the two remaining Wigwam properties on the Mother Road, the Wigwam Motel in Holbrook is a unique lodging experience. Listed on the National Register of Historic Places, this kitschy and original motel allows guests to spend the night in rooms shaped like tipis, adding a touch of nostalgia to the journey.

11. Palo Duro Canyon State Park (Amarillo, Texas): A short 30-minute drive from Amarillo, you'll discover the captivating and breathtaking Palo Duro Canyon State Park. As the second-largest canyon in the United States, it stands as a magnificent natural wonder with its vibrant colors and impressive rock formations. Follow the trails once used by Native

Americans and early Spanish explorers as you hike, bike, or horse ride through this mesmerizing landscape. Don't forget to indulge in a scenic picnic to fully appreciate the awe-inspiring vistas.

12. Lou Mitchell's Diner (Chicago, Illinois): Considered the "First Stop on the Mother Road," Lou Mitchell's is the quintessential all-American diner along Route 66. Established in 1923, three years before Route 66 came into existence, it served as the starting point for hungry drivers about to embark on their journey. Lou Mitchell's is renowned for its hearty breakfasts, fluffy pancakes, prime US burgers, and refreshing fruit shakes that will energize you for the road ahead.

13. Route 66 Museum (Clinton, Oklahoma): Rated as one of the best museums along Route 66, the Route 66 Museum in Clinton offers visitors an immersive journey through the history of this revered highway. Highlights include a replica 1950s diner, a captivating "Dust Bowl" experience, Big Band music from the era, and rotating exhibits that focus on various aspects of Route 66's legacy.

14. Tee Pee Curios Shop (Tucumcari, New Mexico): Hard to miss while driving through Tucumcari, the Tee Pee Curios Shop features colorful concrete wigwams and neon signs. Originally a gas station built in the 1940s, it transformed into a souvenir shop due to the widening of Route 66. Today, it continues to attract passing drivers with its selection of kitsch gifts and Route 66 memorabilia, providing a nostalgic stop along the way.

15. Meramec Caverns (Stanton, Missouri): As one of Missouri's most visited cave systems, Meramec Caverns stands as a highlight landmark for those traversing Route 66. Formed over millions of years through limestone erosion, these 4.6-mile-long caverns hold not only natural wonders but also artifacts dating back to Pre-Columbian Native Americans. Embark on a guided tour to witness the rich history and beauty hidden within these fascinating underground passages.

16. The Gemini Giant (Wilmington, Illinois): Standing at an impressive 30 feet, the Gemini Giant is one of many colossal "Muffler Man" statues found along Route 66. These giant fiberglass models were once utilized as eye-catching advertising for roadside diners and souvenir shops. The Gemini Giant, located in the charming town of Wilmington, advertises the Launchpad Diner and pays homage to the Gemini space program.

17. Sandia Peak Aerial Tramway (Albuquerque, New Mexico): Situated on the eastern edge of Albuquerque, the Sandia Peak Aerial Tramway offers a thrilling 2.7-mile journey over deep canyons and breathtaking terrain. Arriving at the summit, visitors are rewarded with stunning vistas from the observation deck, showcasing the beauty of the Rio Grande Valley and the enchanting Land of Enchantment. Explore the surrounding forest through invigorating hikes, and make sure not to miss the captivating sunset, when the desert sky ignites with a spectacular array of colors and light.

18. Rialto Square Theatre (Joliet, Illinois): Originally opened in 1926 as a vaudeville movie palace, the Rialto Square Theatre is a stunning architectural gem. Designed in the Neo-Baroque style, it boasts dramatic glass chandeliers, intricately painted murals, and gold-flecked marble pillars. Today, the Rialto Square hosts a variety of concerts, musicals, plays, and stand-up comedy shows, providing a perfect opportunity to catch a performance while in Chicago or during your drive to Springfield.

19. Mojave National Preserve (Baker, California): Once you leave the bright lights of Las Vegas behind and cross the Nevada-California border, you'll encounter the expansive Mojave National Preserve. This vast land of deserts, canyons, and rugged mountains offers a wealth of natural beauty. Highlights include witnessing the sunrise or sunset at the Kelso sand dunes, California's second-largest dune system adorned with colorful wildflowers, trekking to Cima Dome, which boasts the world's largest concentration of Joshua Trees, and exploring the stunning limestone Mitchell Caverns.

20. Seligman (Seligman, Arizona): Get your kicks on Route 66 in Seligman, Arizona, and immerse yourself in the retro charm of this Mother Road town. Adorned with neon signs, nostalgic treasures, and classic cars, Seligman evokes a sense of nostalgia. Don't miss Delgadillo's Snow Cap Drive-In, a colorful and kitschy American diner offering a quirky menu featuring items like the "cheeseburger with cheese" and the "dead chicken."

21. Santa Fe (Santa Fe, New Mexico): Founded as a Spanish colony in 1610, Santa Fe, the capital of New Mexico, is renowned for its Pueblo-style architecture and breathtaking views of the Sangre de Cristo Rocky Mountains. While not directly on Route 66, Santa Fe can be explored as a side visit between Amarillo and Albuquerque. Discover the various flea markets, savor margaritas in traditional plazas, and wander along the twisting streets, marveling at the adobe landmarks that define the city's character.

Chapter 27: Best Backpacking Trips In Arizona

The Arizona wilderness boasts a unique and vibrant desert landscape teeming with life. Despite the paradox, it offers a wide range of ecosystems to explore, from majestic mountains and breathtaking canyons to serene waterfall oases and stunning sandstone towers. Arizona is a treasure trove for adventurers, and we are here to help you discover it. We have handpicked four of our favorite backpacking trips in Arizona, providing all the details you need to plan your next unforgettable adventure.

However, it is essential to prioritize safety as Arizona is known for its harsh weather conditions. Make sure to research wildlife information and check weather forecasts before embarking on your journey, ensuring that you are fully aware and adequately prepared.

Important Reminder: Leave No Trace principles are crucial in all outdoor settings, but they hold even more significance for backpacking trips in Arizona's arid climates. The breakdown of food and human waste is inhibited in such environments. Refresh your knowledge of Leave No Trace guidelines and ensure that you pack out whatever you bring in.

Trip	Difficulty	Days	Miles
Grand Canyon Rim to Rim	Moderate	4	24
Havasu Falls	Moderate	2-3	20
Paria Canyon	Moderate	4	38
Superstition Mountains	Strenuous	3	23

Grand Canyon Rim to Rim

Trip Overview
While every trail in the Grand Canyon is awe-inspiring, hiking the Rim to Rim trail stands out as one of the most exceptional backpacking trips in Arizona. This trail grants you the unparalleled opportunity to visit and appreciate both the North and South rims of the canyon. Viewing the Grand Canyon from above is one thing, but immersing yourself in its magnificence by hiking through its depths is an entirely different experience.

Although classified as moderate, hiking down and up the canyon is no easy feat. The descent and ascent are the most challenging parts of the hike, but they are spread out over the course of the journey. Take your training seriously and ensure that you are fully conditioned and prepared before setting out. If you haven't backpacked in the Grand Canyon before, consider registering for a guided Wildland Trekking trip, where you will receive a Grand Canyon-specific packing list.

Trip Details
While it is possible to complete this trail in a single day with a running pace, we recommend taking the time to enjoy and savor the experience. Spacing the hike over a few days makes it easier and infinitely more enjoyable. Typically, this trail takes 4 days and 3 nights to traverse from the North Rim to the South Rim. This itinerary allows for a daily hike of approximately 5-7 miles, giving you ample time to appreciate the surrounding beauty.

Day One:
The Rim to Rim backpacking trip begins on the North Kaibab Trail at the North Rim. You will descend 6.8-7 miles through a dense conifer forest, transitioning into an arid desert landscape. Trekking poles are particularly helpful during the descent, but they are not mandatory.

Day Two:
Continuing the journey, you will hike another 7 miles to reach the Bright Angel Campground. Along the way, you will pass the pristine Ribbon Waterfall.

Day Three:
On the third day, you will embark on a shorter trek of 4.5 miles, leading you to the Havasupai Garden Campground. This leg of the trail holds historical significance for the Native American Havasupai, as you will pass by the Havasupai Garden Spring.

Day Four:
The final day rewards you with breathtaking views of the South Rim as you ascend out of the canyon. From the Havasupai Garden Campground, it is a 4.8-mile journey to the top.

Getting There
Starting at the North Rim, you will likely be coming from Flagstaff, AZ. However, various routes can be taken to reach the North Rim, depending on your starting point. The driving route is well-marked, but for more detailed directions, please refer to the Grand Canyon National Park website.

Permits, Fees, and Reservations
To hike and camp along the Rim to Rim trail, a backcountry permit is required from Grand Canyon National Park. Permit requests should be made in advance, and the permit cost is $10 per permit plus $8 per person

or stock animal per night camped below the rim. For further details and to apply for a permit, visit the Grand Canyon National Park Permit Page.

When to Hike
Spring and autumn are the ideal seasons for hiking the Rim to Rim trail in the Grand Canyon. Summer temperatures can be extreme and make daytime hiking unsafe. Although winter temperatures are tolerable, the North Rim is closed during those months.

Hiking the Grand Canyon with a Guide
Guided backpacking trips for the Grand Canyon Rim to Rim are available, offering a stress-free and exciting way to experience this iconic trail. With a guided tour, permits, gear, transportation, meals, and a professional guide are provided, allowing you to focus entirely on enjoying your adventure. If you choose to book a trip with Wildland Trekking, we highly recommend obtaining trip insurance to cover unforeseen circumstances that may prevent you from embarking on the trek.

Havasu Falls

Trip Overview
Situated on the Havasupai Indian Reservation, the Havasu Falls Trail has gained immense popularity as one of the most sought-after backpacking trips in Arizona. Discovering water in the desert is always a delight, and Havasu Falls serves as a true oasis. Referred to as the "heart of the Grand Canyon," this trail takes you to a part of the canyon inaccessible to bus tours.

Although the trail has some challenging sections, it is overall a moderately rated hike. While it may prove to be quite challenging for first-time backpackers, it remains accessible to most individuals. Keep in mind that this trail has become increasingly crowded over the years due to its popularity. If solitude in the backcountry is what you seek, this may not be the ideal destination. However, once you reach the campsite, there are a few day hikes within the falls area that can provide a respite from the crowds.

Trip Details

In previous years, this hike could be completed in two days with a one-night stay. However, as of 2019, the Havasupai Tribe requires a minimum three-night stay in the falls area. Therefore, most backpackers spend four days exploring this trail and the surrounding falls area.

Day One:

Embarking on an unforgettable journey, you will hike a total of 10 miles on the first day to reach your campsite. The adventure begins at Hualapai Hilltop, where you will descend a series of steep switchbacks. After a 6-mile hike, you will arrive at Havasu Creek. Following the creek for an additional 2 miles, you will reach the village of Supai. From there, it's only 2 more miles until you reach your campground.

During the first day, you will have the opportunity to admire three of the five major waterfalls in the area: Rock Falls, Fifty Foot Falls, and Havasu Falls.

Day Two & Three:

The next two days are dedicated to exploring the falls area and embarking on epic day hikes. One of the highlights is the majestic 200 ft tall Mooney Falls, which is a sight to behold. Don't miss the chance to visit Beaver Falls as well. Take your time to fully immerse yourself in the breathtaking canyon and the multitude of waterfalls along the stream.

Day Four:

As your time in this desert oasis comes to an end, you will retrace your steps and follow the same trail back out of the canyon. Keep in mind that the ascent will involve climbing the steep switchbacks you encountered on the way in. The journey out spans 10 miles.

Getting There:

The trailhead is conveniently located within a 5-hour drive from Phoenix, AZ, Flagstaff, AZ, and Las Vegas, NV. The routes vary depending on your starting point. For detailed driving directions, please refer to the Wildland Trekking website.

Permits, Fees, and Reservations:
A permit is required for this hike, and campground reservations are made for a 3-night/4-day stay. The cost is $100 per person per weeknight and $125 per person per night for the weekend (Friday/Saturday/Sunday nights). Therefore, a 3-night/4-day stay would amount to $300-375. If you wish to stay longer than 3 nights, additional nightly fees apply. Please note that all permit reservations are non-refundable. For more detailed information on making reservations, visit the Havasupai Reservations website.

When To Hike:
Havasu Falls is closed from December to February each year. When choosing the best time of year for your hike, consider your level of experience and preferred temperature range.

Spring is an ideal time, as the snowmelt ensures a continuous flow of water. The days are pleasant, offering longer daylight hours and even opportunities for swimming.

Summer hiking is generally not recommended for most backpacking trips in Arizona. The temperatures at the bottom of the canyon can reach up to 120 degrees Fahrenheit. It is advisable to hike early in the morning and seek shade or swim during the afternoons. July and August are also part of the monsoon season, so be sure to check weather reports. Monsoons can cause flash flooding, making the falls area extremely dangerous.

Autumn offers great potential for an enjoyable backpacking trip to the falls area. Keep in mind that August is still within the monsoon season, so monitor the weather conditions. By late November, temperatures drop significantly and may not be suitable for swimming.

Overall, spring and autumn provide the best hiking conditions, as the temperatures are not dangerously hot. Some hikers do venture to the falls area during summer, but it is crucial to heed heat warnings and carry enough water to sustain you until reaching the campsite. Despite the presence of water and swimming areas near the falls, heat poses a real danger.

Hiking Havasu Falls With A Guide:
This backpacking trip is undoubtedly one of the best in Arizona, and we would love to share the wonders of Havasu Falls with you on a guided trip. However, due to new regulations implemented in 2019, commercial groups are no longer permitted. In the meantime, you have all the information needed to plan an epic adventure on your own!

Trip Overview:
Running parallel to the Arizona-Utah border, the Paria Wilderness area is renowned for its awe-inspiring rock formation known as The Wave. Visiting The Wave requires a permit and offers a fantastic day hike for fortunate permit holders. In close proximity lies the stunning Paria Canyon, featuring a captivating thru-hike that starts at White House, Buckskin Gulch, or Wire Pass Trailhead and ends at Lees Ferry.

This backpacking trip gradually descends around 1,130 feet in elevation, making it a relatively moderate hike. The trail mainly follows the riverbed, ensuring easy navigation. As certain sections of the trail require wading through water, it's important to note that your hiking pace will likely be slower and you may get wet. Prior to entering the canyon, be aware of weather conditions, as flash floods can occur during specific times of the year.

Most backpackers allocate 3-4 days to complete the trail. However, customization is key, as there are numerous campsites along the route. Your personal hiking pace and water levels will determine your daily mileage, and feel free to take your time to fully appreciate the trail. As you meander through the riverbed and canyons, you'll be surrounded by Navajo Sandstone walls reminiscent of Zion's Narrows. Embrace the solitude and marvel at the extraordinary rock formations. It is important to note that when backpacking near a water source or a wash, you must pack out all trash and practice Leave No Trace principles. Additionally, the use of catholes is not permitted, so pack out your toilet paper and human waste in Wag Bags.

Trip Details:
There are three trailhead options for hiking Paria Canyon, but we will focus on the hike starting from White House Trailhead, which spans a distance of 38 miles. Other starting points will result in longer mileage, so take that into consideration when planning your route.

Designated campsites are available along the trail, and there are three reliable springs for water replenishment. Most hikers will not reach the first spring until the second day, so pack accordingly. Although you will be hiking alongside a river, it is not advisable to drink directly from the stream. The silty grit and other water pollutants from upstream may not be effectively filtered by most water filters. It is recommended to filter water directly from the springs.

Day One:
Commencing from the White House Trailhead, your journey will take you along the Paria River for approximately 8 miles until you reach your campsite below the confluence of the Paria River and Buckskin Gulch. Along the way, you'll pass three campsites before reaching mile 7. If you plan to extend your trip beyond 4 days, you can consider stopping at one of these earlier campsites. If you opt to hike to the first water source, you can add 5.2 miles of hiking on the first day.

Day Two:
On the second day, you'll embark on a 12.5-mile hike to a campsite across the river from Wrather Canyon. Along the way, you'll encounter Big Spring, the first reliable water source, so make sure to refill your supplies. The next spring is just under two miles past your campsite, providing additional camping options if needed.

Day Three:
Sticking to the proposed itinerary, you'll have approximately 9.5 miles left to reach your third and final campground, situated on the right-hand side of the river just beyond Bush Head Canyon. Mile 25 marks the Last Reliable Spring, so be sure to refill your water containers before continuing. The remaining trail out of the canyon lacks shade.

Day Four:
Your last day of hiking involves following the riverbed for a final 8 miles until you reach the Lees Ferry Trailhead.

Of course, you have the flexibility to choose the campsites that are located opposite the springs, which can make managing water, particularly for cooking in the evenings, more convenient. Create a plan that suits you and your group, ensuring to bring a map along. With numerous campsites available, you can stop whenever it's practical for you.

Getting There:
The trailhead for this hike is located near Paria Contact Station, just outside of Kanab, Utah. Although the hike begins in Utah, the majority of your time will be spent hiking in Arizona. The Paria Contact Station is situated between mile markers 20 and 21 on Highway 89, positioned between Kanab, UT, and Page, AZ.

Upon completing the trail, you'll need to arrange a shuttle to return to your car. Various shuttle companies are available, with most shuttles from Lees

Ferry to White House Trailhead costing between $200 and $300. If hiking with a group, some groups opt to leave a car at Lees Ferry and drive another car to Paria Contact Station, eliminating the need for a shuttle. This method depends on your starting location.

Permits, Fees, and Reservations:
A permit is required for hiking Paria Canyon and can be applied for online or via phone. Overnight trips require advance permits and cannot be obtained at the Contact Station, although permits for day hikes can be purchased there. Keep in mind that permits are allocated through a lottery system, with only 20 permits distributed per day.

Permits cost $5 per person per night, and an additional nightly charge of $5 applies for bringing dogs into the canyon. Changing a permit incurs a fee of $30 per transaction.

For open dates and permit availability, visit the BLM website.

When To Hike:
Similar to many exceptional backpacking trips in Arizona, the best time to go is during spring and fall. It's advisable to avoid hiking during the period of July to early September due to the risk of flash flooding in the canyon. If planning a hike in early fall, check the weather and consult with rangers for current conditions before setting out.

Although it's possible to hike during the summer months, you'll likely need to allocate more time to avoid the hottest parts of the day. As for winter, keep in mind that a significant portion of the trail involves hiking in water. Fires are not permitted in the canyon, even at campsites, so drying out gear may prove challenging, depending on weather conditions.

Hiking Paria Canyon with a Guide:
Wildland Trekking offers a guided Paria Canyon Backpacking Trip. This comprehensive trip includes permits, gear, meals, and transportation.

Originating and concluding in St. George, Utah, it operates during the spring and fall months. Opting for a guided experience will provide an adventure you'll cherish forever.

White Rock Springs - Superstition Mountains

Trip Overview:
The Superstition Mountains offer a plethora of incredible hiking opportunities, including some of the finest backpacking trips in Arizona. These backpacking trails often connect with various side-trails, allowing you to craft a unique route. With its expansive 160,200-acre area, the Superstition Wilderness boasts over 170 miles of trail networks. While not all trails are equally well-maintained, there are still plenty of options to choose from.

The White Rock Springs figure-eight trail covers a distance of 23 miles round trip, following a network of trails. This hike involves an elevation gain of 3,000 feet and includes sections with loose rock. Hiking poles can be useful, and the overall difficulty level should be considered strenuous.

Important Information: Before embarking on any backpacking or extended day hike in the Superstition Wilderness, it's crucial to contact the Tonto National Forest Mesa Ranger District for an up-to-date backcountry water report.

Trip Details:
Although this backpacking trip is known as White Rock Springs, there is no trail specifically named as such. The name refers to the destination where you intend to reach and camp nearby. Along the route, you'll also be treated to stunning views of Weaver's Needle, an iconic 1,000-foot high feature in the Superstition Wilderness.

Day One:

The first day involves a 7-mile trek, commencing at First Water Trailhead, where you should register. Initially, you'll follow this trail for a short distance of 0.3 miles before reaching a fork. It is recommended to proceed along Second Water Trail (1.5 miles) to Black Mesa Trail (3.3 miles), which leads you past Dutchman's Trail up Bull Pass and around Black Top Mesa (1.5 miles). While you'll reconnect with Dutchman's Trail, do not follow it. Instead, continue straight on a slight descent (0.4 miles) to join Calvary Trail, which will lead you to White Rock Springs and numerous backcountry camping options.

Day Two:
One of the highlights of this backpacking trip is the convenience of having a basecamp. You can leave your camp set-up and embark on a 10-mile hiking loop on day two with just a day pack. It is recommended to hike the loop counterclockwise, allowing you to visit Charlebois Spring during the last mile of the hike. Start by retracing your steps on Dutchman's Trail (1.2 miles) until you reach Terrapin Trail (2.8 miles). Follow this trail until you intersect with Bluff Springs Trail, then continue until you reconnect with Dutchman's Trail (5 miles). From there, it's just one more mile back to camp for the night.

Day Three:
On your way out, retrace your path, but this time continue on Dutchman's Trail all the way to First Water Trailhead. This will be a 6.8-mile hike. Be aware that descending this route may have loose rocks, so it is suggested to use hiking poles.

Getting There:
The First Water Trailhead is located outside of Mesa, AZ, past the Lost Dutchman State Park. If you're coming from the Mesa and Apache Junction area, follow Highway 88 (N Apache Trail) until you can make a right turn onto N 1st Water Road. This will lead you to the trailhead.

Permits, Fees, and Reservations:

Certain recreational activities may require a pass, and a permit/pass is generally necessary for multi-day trips. For more information, visit the Tonto National Forest website.

When To Hike:
It is recommended to hike in the Superstition Mountains during the spring or autumn. Shade is limited, and water is scarce, so summer hiking is not advised, as with most backpacking trips in Arizona. Winter months offer comfortable daytime temperatures, with evenings around 40 degrees. While snow is rare in the Superstition Mountains, it's still essential to keep an eye on the forecast.

Arizona offers a wealth of hiking opportunities, too numerous to list here. But now you know our favorite backpacking trips in the state and have all the information you need for an incredible adventure. From where to go and when to go, to permits, itineraries, and more, everything is right at your fingertips. So what are you waiting for? Get out there and explore.

Wildland Trekking Hiking Adventures:
As the world's premier hiking and trekking company, Wildland specializes in connecting people with amazing environments in fantastic ways. Arizona offers an array of incredible hiking and trekking experiences, including the renowned Grand Canyon. Wildland Trekking offers a variety of multi-day hiking and backpacking adventures throughout Arizona's most breathtaking regions.

Chapter 28: Kayaking In Arizona

Kayaking in Arizona's lakes and rivers is a fantastic way to enjoy the beauty of the area while getting some exercise in a peaceful setting. The state parks in Arizona offer numerous kayaking options in some of the most stunning locations. Discover more about kayaking in Arizona, its benefits, and where you can embark on this wonderful activity in the diverse and gorgeous state!

Benefits of Kayaking for Health

Engaging in low-impact activities like kayaking promotes overall joint and tissue health, reducing the risk of wear and tear.

Kayaking raises heart rate, improving cardiovascular fitness.

The activity strengthens muscles in the torso, shoulders, chest, arms, and back.

Kayaking in serene settings with rhythmic movements promotes relaxation and reduces stress.

Since kayaking is an outdoor activity, it allows your body to absorb more vitamin D from the sun.

Regular kayaking improves stamina and endurance, increasing energy levels over time.

Kayaking Safety

While kayaking provides many benefits, it's important to be aware of safety measures. Follow these tips to ensure a safe and enjoyable kayaking experience:

1. Always wear an approved flotation device while kayaking.
2. Check weather conditions before your trip and avoid kayaking during lightning storms.
3. Dress appropriately for the weather you will encounter.
4. Stay hydrated by drinking plenty of water.
5. Enhance visibility to other watercraft by using reflectors or wearing fluorescent colors on your kayak, clothing, and safety equipment.
6. Kayak within your skill level and avoid unnecessary risks.
7. Before each trip, inspect all kayaking equipment and make any necessary repairs or replacements.

Kayaking Locations in Arizona

Despite being a desert state, Arizona offers a wealth of water recreation opportunities. Lakes and rivers are scattered throughout the state, providing excellent kayaking options, especially within Arizona's state parks. Explore some of the top kayaking spots in different regions of Arizona:

Northern Arizona

Verde River: Enjoy kayaking in various spots in northern Arizona, such as Dead Horse Ranch State Park. This beautiful park features three serene lagoons and access to the Verde River, offering an exciting river kayaking experience.

Fool Hollow Lake Recreation Area: Located in the White Mountains, this park provides the opportunity to kayak on Fool Hollow Lake surrounded by Ponderosa pines and wildlife.

Lyman Lake State Park: Experience the tranquility of kayaking on this expansive high desert lake, enjoying the vastness and peacefulness of the water.

Western Arizona

Lake Havasu State Park: Situated on the Colorado River, this popular park offers kayak rentals and the chance to embark on unforgettable kayaking adventures.

Cattail Cove State Park: Enjoy a low-key boating experience by kayaking on the Colorado River downstream from Lake Havasu. The park provides kayak rentals and lessons for beginners.

Buckskin Mountain and River Island State Parks: These two parks in Parker, Arizona, offer excellent launch spots and kayaking opportunities along the Colorado River.

Southern Arizona

Patagonia Lake State Park: Discover the desert oasis of Patagonia Lake, where you can rent a kayak or bring your own to explore the scenic lake surrounded by southern Arizona's birds, wildlife, and high-desert views.

Roper Lake State Park: Located near Safford, this hidden gem features tule-lined shores and picturesque views of nearby Mt. Graham, providing a memorable kayaking experience.

Kayak Fishing

Kayak fishing allows anglers to access secluded spots that are often unreachable from shore, increasing their chances of catching fish. Kayaking to these secluded areas where fish seek cover, such as reeds, offers a unique fishing experience. Kayaks are an affordable and efficient way to reach prime fishing spots and provide exercise while enjoying the sport.

Catching Fish from a Kayak

To fish for bass from a kayak, paddle near reeds or other areas of fish activity and retrieve your lure to attract the bass. Another effective technique is to flip weedless plastic baits into the reeds and let them fall, repeating the process until you get a bite. During late fall, winter, and early spring, the Arizona Game and Fish Department stocks rainbow trout in several park lakes. Trolling for trout with spinners like RoosterTails or Z-Rays is a popular method from a kayak.

Kayaking in Arizona offers an incredible opportunity to enjoy nature, improve fitness, and indulge in thrilling adventures. Plan your kayaking trip today and make the most of this wonderful activity in the diverse landscapes of Arizona's lakes and rivers.

Chapter 29: Off-Roading In Arizona

Embarking on an off-road adventure in Arizona is an excellent way to discover the vast network of trails, roads, and open areas available for off-highway vehicles (OHVs), motorbikes, and all-terrain vehicles (ATVs).

You can spend your time navigating the iconic red rocks of Sedona or tackling steep, rocky trails that lead to breathtaking desert canyon waterfalls. Alternatively, you may choose to explore the volcanic cinder fields where NASA astronauts once trained or visit abandoned mining towns that transport you back in time. With Arizona's favorable climate, you can enjoy these outdoor escapades year-round.

Important Note: To operate OHVs on public and state trust lands in Arizona, both residents and non-residents must display a valid OHV decal. You can find more information and purchase the necessary decal.

Conquer the sand dunes

For an exhilarating off-road experience, venture into Arizona's sand dunes. Near Yuma and the state's western border, you'll find two popular areas perfect for kicking up some dust.

Take on the Ehrenberg Sandbowl, a vast 2,000-acre site located between Yuma and Lake Havasu City along the Colorado River. This OHV area is open to most types of vehicles and is a favorite among dune buggies and ATVs. About two hours south, you can live out your Star Wars dreams at the massive Imperial Sand Dunes. These dunes were featured in "Episode V: Return of the Jedi" and offer an otherworldly experience.

Both the Ehrenberg Sandbowl and Imperial Dunes require permits, which you can purchase at various gas stations and OHV businesses in the Yuma area, the BLM Yuma Field Office, or online at fareharbor.com/isdpermits (Imperial Sand Dunes only).

On the opposite side of the state lies the Hot Well Dunes Recreation Area near Safford. This unique spot offers not only thrilling rides on the dunes but also the opportunity to relax and soak in the on-site hot tubs.

Rides with added activities and sights
Enhance your off-road adventure by choosing trails that offer more than just scenic views.

Immerse yourself in Arizona's history as you traverse old mining routes in Hualapai Mountain Park near Kingman. For an even more intriguing experience, explore the remnants of the abandoned Swansea mining town east of Parker. Though the glory days of mining are long gone, the few remaining brick buildings, the railroad grade, and the mine shafts provide a fascinating glimpse into the past.

If you enjoy a diverse range of outdoor activities, head to Bulldog Canyon OHV Area near Apache Junction, east of Phoenix. This area offers options for water sports at nearby Saguaro Lake and opportunities for backcountry hiking.

Bulldog Canyon serves as the southernmost point and starting point for Arizona's portion of the Great Western Trail. Stretching 4,455 miles from Mexico to Canada, this backcountry route traverses Montana, Idaho, Utah, and Arizona. In Arizona, the trail covers approximately 300 miles through the picturesque Tonto and Kaibab National Forests, concluding at the Utah border east of Fredonia.

Sit back and enjoy the ride with guided tours
For less-experienced riders or those traveling without their own equipment, various outfitters in Arizona, such as Stellar Adventures, Desert Dog Offroad Adventures (in Phoenix), and Arizona ATV Adventures (in Sedona, Phoenix, and Tucson), offer guided tours with ATVs and knowledgeable guides to accompany you on your exploration.

These guided tour options cover different regions of the state:

- Navigate the trails and historic sites in Box Canyon near Florence, passing through creeks and washes in the rugged Tonto National Forest.
- Start in the lush Verde Valley and ascend 800 miles above the valley floor to Skeleton Bone Mountain for a panoramic view.
- Experience the historic Wild West and admire the desert beauty among the Bradshaw Mountains north of Phoenix.
- Other tours highlight nature and history programs along the rim and within the depths of the majestic Grand Canyon, the magnificent saguaro cacti of the Sonoran Desert, the ancient Indian ruins of Canyon de Chelly, and the less-accessible areas of Monument Valley's extraordinary formations.

Chapter 30: 12 Best Places to Go Shopping in Phoenix

The Phoenix area offers a variety of shopping experiences, including outdoor malls, outlets, farmer's markets, and well-established retail complexes. Whether you're seeking upscale boutiques or great bargains, our guide to the best shopping destinations in Phoenix will help you plan your shopping adventure.

Desert Ridge Marketplace
Located in North Phoenix, the Desert Ridge Marketplace is a spacious outdoor mall covering 110 acres. It's a fantastic destination for shopping, dining, and entertainment. Take a leisurely stroll through popular retail stores like H&M, Old Navy, Kohl's, Target, Barnes & Noble, and Pier 1 Imports.

The marketplace also features an 18-screen movie theater, rock climbing activities, and picturesque outdoor fireplaces and water features. With a variety of dining options, including Chipotle, Jimmy John's, Thirsty Lion, Pigtails Cocktail Bar, and Dave & Buster's, you can refuel after your shopping spree.
Location: 21001 N Tatum Blvd, Phoenix, AZ 85050, USA

Opening Hours: Monday to Saturday from 11 am to 9 pm, Sunday from noon to 6 pm
Phone: +1 480-513-7586

Tanger Outlet Center
Situated in West Phoenix near the Westgate Entertainment District, the Tanger Outlet Center is a must-visit for those in search of discounted designer clothing, jewelry, furniture, and home decor. Browse through a wide range of renowned brands such as H&M, Levi's, Nike, Lululemon, Michael Kors, Calvin Klein, Tommy Hilfiger, and Under Armour. Don't forget to grab discount coupons and a map of the stores from the customer service center.
Location: 6800 N 95th Ave, Glendale, AZ 85305, USA
Opening Hours: Friday to Saturday from 10 am to 9 pm, Sunday to Thursday from 10 am to 8 pm
Phone: +1 623-877-9500

Uptown Farmers' Market
For a foodie's paradise, head to the Uptown Farmers' Market located just 5 miles north of Phoenix's city center. This vibrant market offers an array of vendors selling fresh fruits and vegetables, microgreens, baked goods, homemade salsas, caramel corn, ice cream, and unique varieties of hummus.

Food trucks provide delicious options such as breakfast burritos, quesadillas, tamales, pizza, Thai street food, and Dutch poffertjes (small, fluffy pancakes). In addition to food items, you can shop for Italian olive oils, balsamic vinegar, pet treats, flowers, aprons, turquoise stones, handcrafted soaps, and skincare products.
Location: 5757 N Central Ave, Phoenix, AZ 85012, USA
Opening Hours: Saturday from 7 am to 11 am
Phone: +1 602-859-5648

Downtown Phoenix Farmers Market

Immerse yourself in a vibrant atmosphere at the Downtown Phoenix Farmers Market, boasting over 100 local vendors and growers. Here, you can find farm-fresh fruits and vegetables, eggs, grass-fed meats, baked goods, honey, locally-roasted coffee, homemade salsas, peanut butter, gluten-free and vegan options, as well as handcrafted artisan jewelry and health and wellness products. Indulge in various food truck offerings, including empanadas, Tunisian cuisine, vegan muffins, breakfast burritos, and Persian-style flatbread pizza.
Location: 721 N Central Ave, Phoenix, AZ 85004, USA
Opening Hours: May to October: Saturday from 7 am to 11 am, October to May: Saturday from 8 am to 1 pm
Phone: +1 602-625-6736

Roadrunner Park Farmers Market
Established in 1989, the Roadrunner Park Farmers Market is Phoenix's first and oldest farmers market. Explore a wide range of local farm produce, including fresh fruits and vegetables, baked treats, homemade jams and jellies, and various meats. Some stalls also offer handcrafted items.

Located in the lush Roadrunner Park, you can enjoy the children's playground, observe ducks and geese, or even take a refreshing swim in the public pool after perusing the market. Spread out a blanket and savor your market goodies on the grass.
Location: 3502 E Cactus Rd, Phoenix, AZ 85032, USA
Opening Hours: May to October: Saturday from 7 am to 11 am, October to May: Saturday from 8 am to 1 pm
Phone: +1 623-848-1234

Ahwatukee Farmers Market
The Ahwatukee Farmers Market, situated about 15 miles south of Phoenix's city center, offers a diverse selection of locally grown and produced food. Discover seasonal fruits, vegetables, herbs, freshly baked bread, yogurt, jams, and homemade salsas. Indulge in authentic Southwest and Polish cuisine, brick-fired pizza, fresh coffee, smoothies, or browse

through the selection of jewelry, lotions, soaps, makeup, and candles for unique gifts.
Location: 4700 Warner Rd, Phoenix, AZ 85044, USA
Opening Hours: June to September: Saturday from 8 am to 11 am, October to May: Saturday from 9 am to 1 pm
Phone: +1 623-848-1234

Phoenix Premium Outlets

Located in Chandler, approximately 19 miles southeast of Downtown Phoenix, the Phoenix Premium Outlets offer a delightful open-air shopping experience. With over 90 high-end stores, including DKNY, Armani, Michael Kors, Elie Tahari, Columbia Sportswear, Converse, Gap, and Saks OFF 5th, this outlet is a paradise for shoppers. Enjoy the landscaped surroundings adorned with palm trees, desert flora, and water features, and take a break at the food court.
Location: 4976 Premium Outlet Way, Chandler, AZ 85226, USA
Opening Hours: Monday to Thursday from 11 am to 8 pm, Friday to Saturday from 10 am to 9 pm, Sunday from 10 am to 7 pm
Phone: +1 480-639-1766

Uptown Plaza

Uptown Plaza, a beautifully restored mid-20th-century shopping center in Phoenix, offers a charming mix of locally-owned boutiques, national stores, and a variety of dining options. Take a moment to relax at one of the cafes and enjoy a leisurely walk through the mall.

Visit Muse Apparel for trendy clothing, Local Nomad for unique gifts, West Elm for modern decor, and indulge yourself with a massage or beauty treatment at CLOVR Life Spa. Don't miss Uptown Plaza's Second Saturdays event, which often includes live music, yoga, and kids' activities.
Location: 100 E Camelback Rd, Phoenix, AZ 85012, USA
Opening Hours: Daily from 8 am to 11 pm

Melrose District

The Melrose District is a treasure trove of antique and vintage items, offering some of the best finds in the city. Located along 7th Avenue between south Camelback Avenue and Indian School Road, this 1-mile stretch is lined with boutiques and specialty shops.

Whether you have a passion for retro or modern clothing, books, gifts, music, or furniture, the Melrose District is sure to satisfy your unique taste. Explore Retro Ranch for vintage clothes and accessories, and visit Modern Manor for mid-century furniture. Don't forget to grab a delicious lunch at popular spots like the Fry Bread House, Thai Long-An, or Short Leash Hotdogs & Rollover Doughnuts.

Biltmore Fashion Park
For trendsetters and fashion enthusiasts, the Biltmore Fashion Park is a must-visit shopping destination. This luxurious retail spot is home to high-end boutiques and renowned brands, including Macy's, Saks Fifth Avenue, Ralph Lauren, Hyde Park Jewelers, and Lululemon.

The iconic outdoor lifestyle center features beautiful green lawns, enchanting water fountains, and picturesque pathways. After a satisfying shopping spree, indulge in a delectable meal at dining options like The Capital Grille, Blanco Tacos + Tequila, Seasons 52, or True Food Kitchen. Be sure to stop by the Concierge Desk for a visitor guide and a free Visitor Savings card.
Location: 2502 E Camelback Rd, Phoenix, AZ 85016, USA
Opening Hours: Monday to Saturday from 10 am to 8 pm, Sunday from 11 am to 7 pm
Phone: +1 602-955-8400

Phoenix Public Market
Support local businesses at the Phoenix Public Market, a vibrant hub for farmers, bakeries, coffee shops, and more. Located a few blocks south of the Roosevelt/Central light rail station in Downtown Phoenix, this market

offers a wide array of in-season produce, freshly baked bread and pastries, and locally sourced honey.

Arrive early to savor delicious breakfast sandwiches or visit later for a satisfying lunch in a welcoming atmosphere. If you're driving, keep an eye out for the chalkboard at the entrance that provides directions to free parking lots.
Location: 721 N Central Ave, Phoenix, AZ 85004, USA
Opening Hours: May to September: Saturday from 8 am to noon, October to April: Saturday from 8 am to 1 pm
Phone: +1 602-625-6736

Phoenix Park & Swap
Experience the thrill of bargain hunting at the expansive Phoenix Park & Swap, a massive flea market where locals claim you can find just about anything. Conveniently located at the corner of 40th Street and Washington Street, it's an easy drive from downtown, and parking is always free.

With nearly 50 acres of land and a vast number of vendors, leaving empty-handed is nearly impossible. From clothing and home decor to carnival rides and concession stands, you'll discover a wide range of items. Enjoy the lively festival atmosphere and live music as you spend a delightful afternoon with family and friends. Adults are required to pay an admission fee, but for an even greater deal, visit on Fridays when entry is free for all.

Location: 3801 E Washington St, Phoenix, AZ 85034, USA
Opening Hours: Wednesday from 4 pm to 10 pm, Friday from 6 am to noon, Saturday and Sunday from 6 am to 4 pm
Phone: +1 602-273-1250

Chapter 31: 7 National Parks And Monuments You Might Not Know About, But Should

The United States is renowned for its stunning national parks and monuments. While Rocky Mountain National Park remains my personal favorite, there are many other lesser-known parks and monuments that deserve recognition. In this list, I hope to inspire you to explore these hidden gems, each offering its own unique charm. Over the past year, I had the pleasure of visiting each of these parks, and to my delight, they were not crowded.

If you seek a quieter park experience away from the crowds, this list is perfect for you. Obtain an annual pass from any visitor center, and you won't have to pay daily fees to access these national parks and monuments.

1. Theodore Roosevelt National Park - North Dakota

Situated on the southwestern edge of North Dakota, Theodore Roosevelt National Park encompasses two units. The South Unit's entrance is in the charming town of Medora, while the North Unit is approximately 15 miles south of Watford City, about an hour's drive from Medora. Bison roam freely against the breathtaking backdrop of North Dakota's Badlands. Keep your eyes peeled as you drive through the park, as wild horses often make appearances. Both units offer numerous hiking trails and picturesque photo opportunities.

Medora is conveniently located on I-94, and the North Unit is accessible via Highway 85, a major road in North Dakota. Remember to bring your camera, binoculars, and comfortable hiking shoes. Wildlife sightings are spectacular, and the park boasts both rugged and paved hiking trails with stunning views.

2. Chaco Culture National Historical Park - New Mexico

Located in New Mexico, Chaco Culture National Historical Park requires a journey to reach. I highly recommend bringing an actual map, as GPS is unreliable in this area. Downloading your route before heading to the park is also advisable. While the road to the park is rough, it becomes paved once you enter the park's boundary. We were grateful to be in our four-wheel-drive truck when we drove the 20 miles of rough dirt road. I would not recommend this route for RVs or small cars, although we did spot them along the way. However, the park itself is incredibly beautiful and worth every bump.

The nine-mile loop drive is fantastic, and I encourage you to explore each site you come across. With over 3,000 architectural structures dating back over 1,000 years, the park offers a remarkable sight. The climate is hot and dry, so be sure to carry plenty of water. Paved and rocky hiking trails lead to both the park's main attractions and its rugged areas. If you enjoy history and a bit of a challenge, this national park is sure to captivate you. To experience more comfortable weather, I suggest visiting in fall or spring, as the summer heat can be intense.

3. Mesa Verde National Park - Colorado

Nestled in the southwest corner of Colorado, Mesa Verde National Park was established in 1906 to preserve the archeological heritage of the Ancestral Pueblo people. From 600 to 1300 A.D., this area served as their home. The park boasts over 5,000 archaeological sites, including 600 cliff dwellings, making it a truly awe-inspiring destination. Today, the park safeguards nearly 5,000 known archaeological sites, with 600 cliff dwellings among the most notable and well-preserved in the United States.

Make a stop at the visitor center for the latest park information and to secure tickets for guided tours. While you can explore some cliff dwellings without a special ticket, taking a guided tour enhances your understanding of the people's history. I highly recommend returning to the park at sunset for a mesmerizing experience. Remember to exit the park before dark, as the gates close. Due to the dry climate, it's essential to pack an ample supply of water.

4. Walnut Canyon National Monument - Arizona

Last fall, I stumbled upon Walnut Canyon National Monument while exploring northern Arizona near Flagstaff. It's easily accessible from I-40, and the signs will guide you to this national monument. The canyon itself is breathtaking, surrounded by stunning scenery. Located along the route to the Grand Canyon, it makes for a convenient stop for national park enthusiasts like yourself. The Island Trail, a one-mile hiking trail that takes about an hour to complete, offers views of the area's cliff dwellings. Upon reaching the visitor center, you'll notice an elevator. This elevator provides access to viewpoints not visible from the main entrance, making it helpful for those in need of assistance.

5. Sunset Crater Volcano National Monument - Arizona

Sunset Crater Volcano National Monument, near Flagstaff, provides a unique glimpse into the region's volcanic history. The eruption of Sunset Crater Volcano in 1085 significantly transformed the landscape. Today, visitors can explore the Bonito lava flow and various volcanic features. The drive through this national monument is intriguing, with visible lava tubes and remnants of volcanic ash still displaying vivid colors. The monument connects with Wupatki National Monument, and the entrance fee allows access to both sites.

6. Wupatki National Monument - Arizona

Continuing your drive from Sunset Crater Volcano National Monument, be sure to visit Wupatki National Monument. Stretching across miles of prairie, this area is dotted with ancient pueblos nestled amidst the red rock outcroppings. Witnessing the ancient living spaces of people from long ago is truly fascinating. Numerous roadside parking spots allow you to easily explore these pueblos. You'll be pleasantly surprised by the excellent condition of some of the structures. Set aside approximately three hours to fully appreciate both national monuments, and consider packing a picnic lunch to extend your time in these beautiful parks.

7. Effigy Mounds National Monument - Iowa

Located along the Great River Road in eastern Iowa, Effigy Mounds National Monument showcases over 200 Native American mounds. Many consider these mounds sacred, particularly the members of the monument's 20 culturally associated Native American tribes. A visit offers an opportunity to reflect on the mounds' significance and the people who constructed them. The mounds, shaped like birds, bears, deer, bison, lynx, turtles, panthers, and water spirits, are abundant in this picturesque section of the Upper Mississippi River Valley.

The mounds were primarily built for burial purposes, setting them apart from many other mounds found across the country. Unlike others, these mounds were not intended for storing trade goods. Plan to spend approximately three hours in this park and pack a picnic lunch. Fall offers particularly stunning views, as the foliage displays vibrant colors. Iowa boasts numerous hiking trails, including several in this area of the state.

Chapter 32: 20 Ghost Towns In Arizona

Arizona's ghost towns hold a distinct appeal for urban explorers and history enthusiasts alike. These abandoned locations offer a chance to step back in time and delve into the region's rich past. Arizona boasts one of the largest collections of ghost towns in the United States, owing to the combination of mining towns being abandoned when the mines ran dry and the favorable dry conditions for preservation.

Despite their allure, many of these ghost towns remain hidden gems, either due to their remote locations or their state of disrepair, deterring visitors. Our carefully curated list of Arizona's finest ghost towns ensures a rewarding experience for those seeking to immerse themselves in the "Grand Canyon State's" captivating history.

1. GOLDFIELD GHOST TOWN & MINE

Situated approximately 10 miles (16 kilometers) east of Scottsdale, the Goldfield Ghost Town & Mine was established in the 1890s. While not completely deserted like most ghost towns, it was abandoned in 1926. Today, the town has been meticulously restored to retain its Wild West spirit and provide an immersive historical experience. Visitors can indulge in activities such as horseback riding, exploring museums, browsing gift shops, enjoying a drink at a historic saloon, and even embarking on a thrilling zipline adventure. The town also offers tours of old gold mines, gold panning experiences, and a shooting range for those seeking excitement. Goldfield Ghost Town & Mine is located at 4650 North Mammoth Mine Road, Apache Junction, Arizona, 85119.

2. TOMBSTONE

Tombstone, one of Arizona's most renowned ghost towns, was founded in 1877 and is situated southeast of Tucson. Originally a bustling mining town, it experienced a rapid decline in 1892 when the mines were depleted. Nevertheless, Tombstone remains the largest Wild West town still in existence, having been meticulously restored and transformed into a popular tourist attraction. Visitors can explore legendary sites such as the O.K. Corral, historic saloons, cemeteries, theaters, parks, churches, and various other well-preserved buildings. Museums, art galleries, historic gold mine tours, and a Wild West-themed amusement park further enhance the town's allure. Tombstone truly offers an unparalleled experience of the Old West.

3. VULTURE CITY GHOST TOWN

Located northwest of Phoenix, on the site of the historic Vulture Mine—Arizona's largest gold mine—Vulture City Ghost Town presents visitors with a glimpse into the past. Established in 1863, the town thrived until 1942, when the mine was abandoned due to depletion. Despite falling into disrepair, many of the town's buildings have been restored and preserved for future generations. Today, visitors can explore the stone and adobe structures that once housed saloons, gas stations, brothels, homes, hotels, offices, storehouses, workers' residences, and mess halls. For a more immersive experience, a guided walking tour of the mine is available. Vulture City Ghost Town can be found at 36610 355th Avenue, Wickenburg, Arizona, 85390.

4. GOLD KING GHOST TOWN & MINE

Nestled near Jerome, between the Coconino and Prescott National Forests, Gold King Ghost Town & Mine features a small collection of weathered buildings, vintage cars and trucks, and remnants of the mine itself. Some buildings have been adorned with artifacts dating back over a century, creating an authentic atmosphere. Despite receiving fewer visitors than it deserves, this hidden gem offers a delightful experience. Gold King Ghost Town & Mine can be found at Perkinsville Road, Jerome, Arizona, 86331. Additionally, a guided ghost walk in Jerome provides an opportunity to hunt for ghosts using EMF readers and Spirit Boxes.

5. HACKBERRY

Located along the historic Route 66, Hackberry was initially established as a mining town in 1874. Though largely abandoned in 1919, it still maintains a small population. The town's legacy in the motor industry is reflected in its collection of historic cars, garages, gas stations, and fuel pumps. Visitors can immerse themselves in the town's history by exploring attractions like the general store, music hall, motel, and a 1920s coal kiln. Hackberry offers a unique experience of a historic Southwest town.

6. BISBEE

Situated near the Mexican border, Bisbee distinguishes itself from most ghost towns due to its relatively large population. However, it qualifies as a ghost town due to its significant historical sites that preserve its mining town heritage. Visitors can explore attractions such as the Bisbee Mining & Historical Museum, Bisbee Restoration Museum, Copper Queen Mine, Central School, and the Lavender Pit. These sites offer insights into the town's structures, history, and industries, exemplifying how a former mining town can evolve instead of fading into oblivion.

7. FAIRBANK

Founded in 1881, Fairbank played a crucial role as the closest rail station to Tombstone and the nearest stagecoach station to Bisbee. This made it a vital link between the two towns. Fairbank reached its peak popularity in the 1920s but declined when nearby mines began closing. Finally abandoned in the 1970s, it epitomizes the definition of a ghost town, with dilapidated buildings and no residents remaining. Visitors can explore remnants such as a general store, saloon, post office, hotel, schoolhouse, stable, outhouse, railroad bridges and platforms, along with a few houses.

8. OATMAN

Established around 1910, Oatman experienced a rapid boom in 1915 when more than $10 million worth of gold was discovered. The town flourished for almost five decades before the mines ran dry, leading to its near abandonment. Today, Oatman relies on its historical significance and its proximity to Route 66 for survival. Visitors can explore historic buildings, remnants of the mines, and enjoy picturesque views of Route 66 from the surrounding hills. Unique encounters with wild burros and handcrafted souvenirs available at the local gift shop further enhance the town's charm.

9. CHLORIDE

Originally founded in 1863 as a silver mining camp, Chloride holds the distinction of being Arizona's oldest continually inhabited mining town and home to the state's oldest continually operated post office. Unfortunately, a fire in the late 1920s ravaged much of the town. Today, visitors can explore a small collection of mines and buildings, including a playhouse and jail. The surrounding area boasts brightly colored painted boulders, creating a unique mural for exploration.

10. GLEESON

Originally known as Turquoise and founded in 1875, Gleeson thrived as a copper mining town until the mines dried up in 1939 during World War II. Subsequently, the town was all but abandoned. Visitors can discover remnants of a cemetery, hospital, jail, saloon, school foundations, and evidence of mining activities. A small population still resides in Gleeson, offering handcrafted rattlesnake products and adding to the town's distinctive ambiance.

11. SWANSEA

Located near the California border, Swansea was a small ghost town that existed for only 30 years in the early 1900s. Vandalism and weathering have taken their toll on many of the town's sites, but remains of adobe buildings, cemeteries, mine shafts, homes, vintage cars, and foundations provide an eerie yet captivating destination for ghost town enthusiasts to explore.

12. TIP TOP MINE / GILLETT

Located in the hills northwest of Phoenix, Tip Top Mine and Gillet form a pair of ghost towns worth exploring. Tip Top Mine features remnants of the mine and several small buildings, while Gillet boasts what remains of the historic 1878 Burfind Hotel. Together, they offer unique sites for ghost town enthusiasts to enjoy.

13. AGUA CALIENTE

Established in 1744 near hot springs that gave it its name, Agua Caliente started as a small town and eventually grew into a ranch and resort with a 22-room hotel and swimming pool. Unfortunately, it closed when the hot spring waters dried up. While some of its 2,700-acre area remains as farmland, most of it is unkempt and abandoned. With its vast size and collection of ruined buildings, including the hotel, caretaker's quarters, a stone house, store, and other dilapidated sites, Agua Caliente is an incredible place to explore.

14. TWO GUNS

Situated off Route 66 on the edge of the Navajo Nation, Two Guns is a tiny ghost town that makes for an interesting stop while visiting other attractions. With the remains of a campground, trading post, zoo, old cottages, and a burned-out service station, Two Guns showcases the decline of a town that was thriving as recently as the 1970s. Nearby attractions like the abandoned Canyon Diablo Bridge and Apache Death Cave add to the allure.

15. SENECA LAKE

Rather than a town, Seneca Lake is an abandoned summer camp from the 1970s. Although time and vandalism have taken their toll, it still offers an exciting visit amidst stunning natural beauty. Fans of the horror classic Friday The 13th will particularly enjoy the atmosphere.

16. RUBY

Founded in 1877 as the Montana Camp, Ruby was a prosperous mining town known for its diverse metals. However, it gained infamy due to the Ruby Murders and subsequent manhunt in the 1920s. Today, Ruby stands as one of the best-preserved ghost towns in the state, with a range of complete buildings to explore. From a jail and school to houses and a fully equipped mine building, the town offers a glimpse into the past.

17. KENTUCKY CAMP

Established in 1905 as a mining camp, Kentucky Camp lasted a mere seven years before being abandoned. Designated as a historic district in Sonoita and listed on the U.S. National Register Of Historic Places since 1995, Kentucky Camp showcases well-preserved structures and artifacts, providing insights into the area's past. The United States Forest Service ensures the maintenance of its buildings, adding to the allure of the site.

18. NOTHING

One of the state's youngest ghost towns, Nothing was established in 1977 and has been uninhabited since 2005. With a population never exceeding four people, the main sites in Nothing include a gas station, convenience store, and several other dilapidated structures. Despite its brevity, Nothing offers a unique place to stop by the highway.

19. CASTLE DOME LANDING

Settled in 1863 as a mining and railroad camp, Castle Dome Landing played a vital role as a port for steamboats on the Colorado River. The town's mines also provided lead during the two world wars, ensuring its longevity compared to other mining towns. Although the town was eventually abandoned in 1978 and the port submerged, Castle Dome Landing now serves as a living museum. Over 50 buildings have been restored to their 1878 appearance, complete with mannequins and artifacts that bring the stories of the past to life.

20. CORDES

Founded in 1883 by John Henry Cordes, the town of Cordes began emptying in the 1940s and was completely abandoned by 1950. While only a few buildings remain standing, it is said that descendants of the town's founder still reside in the area. Cordes may be a small ghost town, but its haunting atmosphere captivates visitors.

Chapter 33: Is Monument Valley Worth It?

Renowned for its majestic sandstone buttes, breathtaking vistas, and colossal mesas, Monument Valley stands as one of the most iconic landscapes in the United States.

Although its remote location initially deters some tourists, Monument Valley is an absolute must-visit destination. It offers much more than mere rocks in the middle of nowhere. From scenic drives and hiking trails to cultural attractions and informative guided tours, there is something for everyone at Monument Valley.

To help you decide whether to visit this remarkable location, we have outlined its best features and provided insights into exploring it both independently and with a guided tour.

Monument Valley: A Natural Wonder

Monument Valley is a stunning desert region situated on the border of Arizona and Utah. Its most distinctive features are the towering sandstone formations that dominate the landscape.

While Monument Valley was relatively unknown until the 1930s, it gained significant attention in Hollywood films, including Forrest Gump and Mission Impossible: II. This exposure brought about tremendous economic growth, transforming the valley into a popular tourist destination.

Even before its Hollywood debut, Monument Valley held deep significance for the native Navajo people, who refer to it as Tsé Bii' Ndzisgaii, meaning "valley of the rocks." While not officially a national park or monument, it is part of the Navajo Nation's Monument Valley Park.

Things to Do in Monument Valley
While you can catch a glimpse of Monument Valley by driving along U.S. Route 163, truly immersing yourself in its splendor requires paying the entrance fee and exploring its scenic landscape, hiking trails, and various attractions. The valley offers a wealth of experiences; here are just a few highlights:

Marvel at the Rock Formations: Monument Valley's sandstone buttes, with their flat tops and majestic appearance, are a sight to behold. Ranging in height from 400 to 1000 feet (120 to 300 meters), these formations include the famous Mitten Buttes, Merrick Butte, and Totem Pole.

Explore the Valley on the Wildcat Trail: The Wildcat Trail is a self-guided 4-mile loop that takes you through iconic rock formations, such as Merrick Butte and the Mitten Buttes. It offers a scenic hike of approximately 2 to 3 hours.

Discover History at Goulding's Trading Post Museum: For a firsthand glimpse into the trading and cultural history of the Navajos and other Native Americans, visit Goulding's Trading Post Museum. Here, you can view the showroom where locals once traded goods, as well as artifacts, photographs, and movie props from Western films shot in the area.

Independent Exploration in Monument Valley

Exploring Monument Valley on your own can be highly rewarding, particularly if you prefer having control over your tour and the freedom to explore at your own pace. Simply paying the park entrance fee allows access to most of the region's breathtaking landscapes.

While much of the valley can be explored independently, there is only one hiking trail accessible without a guide: the Wildcat Trail. Additionally, a driving trail can be undertaken with the help of a free map obtained from the Visitors Center.

Visiting the main attractions in Monument Valley typically takes around 2 to 4 hours. However, if time permits, exploring the lesser-known attractions in the valley is highly recommended.

Guided Tours of Monument Valley

Guided tours are a popular choice for experiencing Monument Valley. Similar to our Bryce Canyon tour, there are several highly beneficial guided tours available for Monument Valley.

Guided tours offer the advantage of seamless planning and transportation, allowing you to fully enjoy the experience. Some tours even offer comprehensive 3-day trips to Monument Valley, the Grand Canyon, and more, with itineraries tailored to your preferences.

On a guided tour, you can delve deeper into the rich local culture of the Navajo Nation. Additionally, tour guides provide insights into the region's fascinating rock formations and other interesting facts as you traverse the valley. They can also take you to lesser-known locations beyond the typical tourist routes.

Whether you prefer independent exploration or a guided tour, there is an option to suit every type of traveler in Monument Valley.

In Conclusion

Monument Valley is a destination that should not be missed, whether you choose to explore it independently or with a guided tour. Its captivating red rock formations, sandy plains, and desert landscapes have made it the backdrop for countless iconic films. This unique and magical region is sure to leave a lasting impression on anyone who visits.

So, don't hesitate any longer. Start planning your trip to Monument Valley with MaxTour today and prepare for an unforgettable experience!

Chapter 34: Monument Valley Guided Jeep Tours

Butte after butte and mesas upon mesas beckon you to explore. For an unforgettable adventure, we highly recommend the Valley Drive in Monument Valley Navajo Tribal Park. This rough 17-mile dirt road leads to 11 breathtaking viewing points. You may recognize some of these iconic vistas from classic American Western films directed by John Ford and starring John Wayne. Keep in mind that this scenic drive is inaccessible to tour buses, motorcycles, low riders, and certain passenger vehicles.

Fortunately, there are several jeep and van tours available for purchase within the park. These tours often include guided hikes and side trips to exclusive destinations that can only be accessed with a licensed guide. Before embarking on your tour, take some time to explore the visitor center's museum and gift shop. Inquire inside or at the sheds in the parking lot about available trips. You can book a tour of Valley Drive or opt for a longer adventure like Mystery Valley, a highly popular attraction accessible only with a licensed guide. During these tours, you'll travel in a specially designed 4x4 Jeep, perfect for off-road viewing excursions.

These tours offer a fantastic way to experience the surrounding landscape and immerse yourself in Navajo spirit and culture. They are ideal for families, as both kids and adults can enjoy the bouncy Jeep rides and shorter tour durations. Don't forget to bring your camera to capture plenty of memorable photos.

What Sets it Apart
While nothing can truly replace the awe-inspiring solitude of hiking around the sandstone monoliths on trails like the Wildcat Loop Trail, a Jeep tour is an excellent way to discover hidden gems you might have otherwise missed. Cruising along the dusty roads in the park's remote corners and enjoying the exhilarating bumps is undeniably fun.

If your tour takes you on the Valley Drive, you'll pass by and potentially stop at 11 distinct scenic viewpoints. These locations offer incredible opportunities to capture the park's stunning landscapes and rock formations in photographs. It's worth noting that if you take photos of the local Navajo people, a tip is expected.

Most other tours venture off the beaten path, although the exact itinerary depends on the tour operator and the specific trip you choose. Frequently, these tours venture deep into the park and include stops for walks to petroglyphs, arches, and other fascinating sites. Mystery Canyon is one of these majestic areas, and exploring such off-the-grid locations with a knowledgeable guide ensures an unforgettable experience.

Jeep and van tours can be booked in advance or on the day of your visit. Trips depart throughout the day, with the last departures taking place approximately one to two hours before the park closes (specific times vary depending on the season). You can hire a guide in the parking lot at the visitor center or from Goulding's Lodge. Additionally, there are many other native-owned guide companies and outfitters in the area.

Memorable Highlights
The bumpy bliss of traveling to remote locations accessible only with a guide, the captivating tales of history and Native American mythology shared by your guide, and the opportunity to witness the most beautiful and iconic parks in the country—these are just a few of the memories you'll take away from your tour. In a short amount of time, you'll experience the essence of the West, as seen in silver screen classics, and encounter the sacred lands that make Monument Valley truly special. It's easy to understand why filmmaker John Ford fell in love with this place and why John Wayne once said that Monument Valley is "where God put the West."

GPS Coordinates, Parking, and Regulations
GPS Coordinates:
(36.985135, -110.113800)

Park your vehicle at the visitor center, where you'll find numerous guide services offering trips. If you choose a service located elsewhere, such as Goulding's Lodge, follow the parking instructions provided by the service provider.

The best time to visit for optimal comfort is March through early June and October through September. Summer months can be excessively hot, even for jeep travel. You can enjoy tours at any time of day to experience the spectacular views, but if possible, aim for a sunset tour. The long shadows and vibrant red hues create a truly unforgettable experience, especially if you conclude the tour at the lookout point above the Mittens.

The entrance fee for Monument Valley Navajo Tribal Park is $20 per vehicle for up to four people, with an additional fee of $6 per person for any additional occupants. Tour prices range from $40 and up. Dogs are allowed in the park but must be leashed at all times. Check with specific tour operators to determine if dogs are permitted on their tours.

To fully explore Monument Valley, consider reviewing the list of Jeep Tour Operators. Some operators may offer discounts for combining tours.

Goosenecks State Park
Mexican Hat, UT

Located north of Mexican Hat, Goosenecks State Park is easily accessible and offers a million-dollar view. The San Juan River begins in the Colorado mountains and flows until it meets the Colorado River at Lake Powell.

Hiking the Wildcat Trail
Oljato-Monument Valley, UT

The Wildcat Trail is a 3.2-mile loop hike (4 miles total, including the return) that leads you through one of Monument Valley's most scenic areas. This trail will make you feel like you've stepped back in time into the Wild West.

Valley of the Gods
Mexican Hat, UT

Among the intriguing destinations in San Juan County, the Valley of the Gods stands out with its captivating name. Situated near Bears Ears National Monument and Mexican Hat, Utah, this special area attracts visitors looking for idyllic sandstone formations.

Chapter 35: 13 Hot Springs in Arizona Where You Can Soak It All In

The cool desert air embraces you as the sun sets, and mist dances above the hot water, drifting through the cacti. It may sound unusual, but hot springs in the Arizona desert provide the perfect relaxation after a day of adventure. Thanks to ancient volcanic activity in the region's geological history, Arizona is blessed with a variety of hot springs.

But is it a good idea to soak in a hot spring in a hot Southwestern destination like Arizona? During my visit to Jordan, I learned the phrase "when it's hot, you drink hot," referring to the tradition of enjoying hot mint tea regardless of the weather or time of day. I believe the same principle applies to hot springs in a hot climate like Arizona – there's never a bad time to indulge.

If the idea appeals to you, continue reading for a list of the best hot springs in Arizona. While not all are suitable for soaking (some are actually too hot!), you'll discover a range of options that are sure to pique your interest.

1. Arizona Hot Spring

Among all the hot springs in Arizona, Arizona Hot Spring, also known as Ringbolt Hot Spring, holds the highest fame. Situated in the Lake Mead Recreation Area, reaching this hot spring is an adventure in itself. You can either embark on a 2.5-mile hike or enjoy a scenic boat ride along the Colorado River. Your reward awaits at the end – multiple pools with water temperatures reaching 110°F and a magnificent 25-foot waterfall.

2. Castle Hot Springs Resort

Castle Hot Springs Resort stands apart from other hot springs in Arizona for two reasons. Firstly, it is a resort where you can stay overnight, savor farm-to-table meals, and complement your hot spring experience with rejuvenating spa treatments. Secondly, it boasts the title of the hottest non-volcanic natural hot spring in the world!

3. Clifton Hot Springs

Clifton Hot Springs is a hidden gem worth discovering. Located in the town of Clifton, this hot spring was once a favored relaxation spot for soldiers and miners. Although plans to convert it into a bathhouse fell through in the early 20th century, you can still visit these naturally heated pools today.

4. El Dorado Hot Springs

Just an hour's drive from Phoenix, El Dorado Hot Springs is a popular day trip from the state capital. Here, you can soak in stone pools and porcelain clawfoot bathtubs filled with water naturally heated to a comfortable 107°F. If you're feeling adventurous, there's even a clothing-optional section to explore.

5. Essence Of Tranquility

For a simple and off-the-radar getaway, Essence of Tranquility is the place to be. Book a casual casita for a night and spend your entire day indulging in the hot springs. With five private stone pools and one communal pool, you have a variety of options to choose from. Plus, if you call ahead, you can enhance your day with a spa treatment.

6. Gillard Hot Springs

Gillard Hot Springs is a location where it's best to admire from afar. With water temperatures exceeding 180°F, taking a dip is not advisable as it can cause severe burns. Instead, revel in the beauty of the canyon walls and vibrant green trees surrounding Gillard Hot Springs.

7. Hannah Hot Spring

Hannah Hot Spring may be one of the most secluded hot springs in Arizona. To reach this enchanting natural wonder, you'll need to embark on an 8.3-mile hike through a challenging canyon trail. However, your efforts will be rewarded with an amazing hot spring pool boasting water temperatures of 133°F. The best part? You'll likely have this hot spring all to yourself!

8. Hot Well Dunes Hot Springs

While most people visit Hot Well Dunes Recreation Area for off-roading and camping, it also houses the hidden Hot Well Dunes Hot Springs. This tranquil oasis features two cement pools with water naturally heated to a delightful 106°F. Be prepared to put your off-roading skills into action to reach this secluded spot.

9. Kachina Mineral Springs

Situated in the charming town of Safford, Kachina Mineral Springs is one of six hot springs in the area. What sets it apart is the opportunity to enjoy a variety of spa treatments alongside your hot spring soak. Treat yourself to a massage, sweat wrap, or reflexology session for the ultimate relaxation experience.

10. Kaiser Hot Springs

Kaiser Hot Springs is a local favorite. To reach this remarkable hot spring in Arizona, you'll need to conquer a 1.5-mile hike (note that the trail is not well marked). The shallow pool, with temperatures around 100°F, makes the effort worthwhile.

11. Lost Man Hot Spring

Located near the Nevada-Arizona border, just a few miles south of the Hoover Dam, Lost Man Hot Spring remains relatively undiscovered despite its proximity to a major tourist attraction. Journey to this hidden gem and revel in the tranquility it offers.

12. Pumpkin Spring

Pumpkin Spring, located within the Grand Canyon, is both the coolest and most hazardous spot on our list. Its bright orange rock formations resemble pumpkins, but unfortunately, swimming is not permitted due to high levels of arsenic, lead, zinc, and copper. Nonetheless, it provides a stunning backdrop for capturing unforgettable photos.

13. Verde Hot Spring

Verde Hot Spring is undoubtedly one of the most renowned hot springs in Arizona. Located within driving distance of Sedona, Flagstaff, and Prescott, it attracts hundreds of visitors each year who come to enjoy the 102°F waters.

Please note that Verde Hot Springs may sometimes be inaccessible due to dangerous weather and road conditions.

Chapter 36: Everything To Know About Visiting Havasu Falls in 2023

Ever wondered about the stunning blue color of Havasupai Falls? It's all thanks to the minerals present in the water, such as calcium carbonate and magnesium, as well as the Havasu Creek, which washes away the silt. This unique combination creates a breathtaking contrast of baby blue against the orange canyon, making it a sight to behold for hikers who are willing to undertake the 10-mile journey.

To help you prepare for your hike to Havasu Falls, here is a comprehensive guide that covers everything from the permitting process to packing efficiently for your expedition. Are you ready? Let's dive in and explore the 14 key things to know about hiking to Havasu Falls, including some valuable lessons I learned along the way so you can avoid the same pitfalls.

1. Havasu Falls is located on the Havasupai Reservation

The name "Havasu Pai" translates to "people of the blue-green water," reflecting the deep connection the tribe has with the water flowing through their land. The Havasupai tribe has resided in the Grand Canyon for over 800 years. Initially restricted to a small area, they have since regained a significant portion of their homeland. The falls are situated within their reservation, which necessitates obtaining permits to visit.

2. Permits are required

To visit Havasu Falls, you must secure a 3-day permit. Day hikes or alternative durations are not allowed. Permits sell out quickly and can only be booked online. Due to the closure of the canyon during the pandemic, 2023 permits will be issued to current permit holders who must reapply for specific time slots when reservations open on February 1st. Ensure that you have access to your account on the Havasupai Reservations website prior to that date. Be ready to click the permit sales button when it illuminates at 8am Arizona time on February 1st.

If you haven't reserved a permit, don't despair! The website regularly lists "canceled/transferred" permits available at 8am MST each day. It's worth trying your luck as there are usually plenty of permits up for grabs. You'll need to create an account on the site for this purpose.

During my own experience, I logged on promptly at 8am and it took about 2 hours to secure my permit in 2019. The website crashed several times, requiring me to refresh the page around 20 times before I succeeded. By then, only a few dates were available, so I took what I could get and ended up with a late March reservation.

3. Choose the right season

Havasu Falls permits are available from February through November, with peak season falling between May and September. The monsoon season occurs from July to August, which brings the possibility of evacuation. Consider the following factors:

- February to April: These months offer cooler temperatures, which may deter swimming. Hiking is more comfortable during this time as most of the trail is exposed to the sun.
- May to June: The weather is slightly warmer, but it can also be more buggy. In June, average temperatures reach 96°F/36°C.
- July to August: These months bring the hottest temperatures, with an average of 99°F/37°C at Havasupai. It is also the monsoon season, although it is surprisingly popular for permits. Personally, I couldn't imagine backpacking in such hot weather, so it wasn't an option for me. In case of flash floods, permits may be canceled without rebooking or refunds.
- September to November: September can still be quite hot, but as October and November approach, temperatures cool down, potentially making swimming uncomfortable. Choose these months based on the year's weather conditions.

In conclusion, the optimal times to visit are April, May, and October, offering moderate heat that still entices you to take a dip.

Keep in mind that rain doesn't necessarily mean the canyon will be closed. During my hike, it rained, but the clouds passed, and everything was fine. Flash floods are more likely in the summer months when the region is drier, and the ground is less able to absorb stormwater.

4. What to expect on the hike

The hike to Havasu Falls from the trailhead spans 10 miles. The trail is relatively easy to navigate and winds through a picturesque orange canyon. You'll cover 8 miles to reach the town of Supai for check-in, and an additional 2 miles from there to the campground and Havasu Falls.

I was surprised to find the hike rated as "difficult" on my AllTrails app. Since it's mostly flat, I initially thought reviewers were being overly dramatic. The hike down, assuming you're not doing it in scorching heat, is relatively easy. It starts with switchbacks (though not as challenging as those in Zion National Park, if you're familiar) and gradually descends until you reach Supai. Afterward, the trail becomes slightly steeper until you reach Supai Falls and the first campground.

On the return hike, I found it more challenging. The slight incline became more strenuous due to the terrain, which consists mostly of sand and rocks. It was my first time getting a blister in my hiking shoes due to the rocky terrain and constant foot movement. I also didn't time it right. If you hike in the midday heat, you'll be exposed to the sun. Given the 10-mile distance, it's difficult to avoid midday sun exposure, which is why I can't envision attempting this hike in the summer months.

The final switchbacks on the way out are not overly challenging either. If you're not accustomed to hiking or backpacking, they might feel tough, but if you hike regularly, you'll manage just fine.

Here are a few important points to keep in mind:

- Begin your hike as early as possible to avoid the heat. If you can't start early, aim for the afternoon while still allowing enough time to reach your destination before dark.
- The hike to Havasu Falls typically takes 4-7 hours, while the return hike takes 5-8 hours. In my case, it took 4 hours on the way in and 5 hours on the way out, with breaks and a steady pace.
- There is little to no shade along the trail, so plan your hike to take advantage of the shadows cast by the canyon walls. Don't forget to bring sunscreen and wear a hat for sun protection.
- Hiking poles can be helpful for stability on the rocky terrain and during the switchbacks.
- There is minimal water available on the trail, so make sure to carry your own. I recommend bringing a minimum of 2 liters per person on the way

down and 3 liters on the way up during the hotter months. Adjust these amounts slightly for shoulder seasons.

5. Exploring Options for Gear Transportation
If you prefer not to carry all of your gear, there are alternative options available. You can arrange for a mule to transport most of your camping equipment and food down to the site. The cost is $400 round-trip per mule, and each mule can carry up to four bags weighing a maximum of 32 lbs (14.5 kg) per bag. You can reserve the mules when booking your permits through the same website.

However, if you're an animal lover, I strongly recommend packing light and carrying your own gear. There have been reports suggesting that these animals do not have the best living conditions, considering the challenging journey over rocky terrain in extreme heat. For this reason, I chose to carry my own pack. In the next section, I'll provide tips on how to reduce your load and make backpacking easier.

Finally, there's also a helicopter option available. Although it's unlikely you ended up with this book with an interest in flying in or out, I'll mention that you can fly for $85 per person one way, on a first-come, first-served basis. While their website doesn't provide detailed information, I assume you would need to arrange for your gear to be transported separately.

6. Packing Essentials and Preparations
Here's a comprehensive backpacking checklist that includes all of my tried and tested gear.

There are a few additional considerations specific to Havasu Falls:

- It's advisable to pack a second pair of amphibious shoes. You'll encounter several waterfall crossings if you plan to visit Beaver Falls, and repeatedly removing and putting on hiking boots can be tiresome. Opt for a pair that covers your toes, provides traction, and is lightweight. Personally, I found this pair to be excellent:

- I observed around 50 partially used gas cans left behind on the rangers' table, which seemed to serve as a communal supply area. While it may be risky to rely on accessing fuel down there, it's worth considering if needed.

- Remember to pack out all of your trash, so make conscious choices when selecting your food supplies.

- Don't forget to bring a bathing suit and a microfiber towel.

7. Navigating the Food Situation
For the most part, you'll need to bring your own food to the campsite and plan for a three-day stay. However, there are a few food options along the way (with some uncertainty).

Your first option will be a small café located at the beginning of Supai, 8 miles in. The slightly faded sign claims it to be "world-famous," so it might be worth a try. They serve burgers, sandwiches, and other fast food items. It's possible to find items like Gatorade there, although availability may vary.

As you continue further, you'll come across several stands that may or may not be staffed. These stands offer items like nachos, fry bread, and Indian tacos (ground meat served with fry bread). While I can only speculate, "fry bread" seems to be what it sounds like, although I haven't personally tried it.

Keep in mind that snack availability can be unpredictable. There's a humorous sign at one of the stands indicating their opening time as 9:30, but they may or may not be present at 10:30 and might start serving around 12:30. So, while it's not guaranteed, it can be a pleasant surprise if they are open.

8. Selecting a Campsite

The campsite stretches from the base of Havasu Falls to the top of Mooney Falls. You have the freedom to choose your camping spot, but there are a few factors to consider:

- You can either cross a bridge to camp on an island or opt to camp near one of the canyon walls.
- Campsites are available on a first-come, first-served basis.
- Bathroom facilities are located at the entrance, middle, and end of the campsite. Based on my experience, the bathrooms at the entrance seemed to receive more frequent maintenance. They were cleaner and more likely to have toilet paper.
- The bathrooms consist of drop toilets, so there are no showers or running water available. Please adhere to the leave no trace principles by using the facilities appropriately and disposing of gray water from toothbrushing or cooking far away from water sources, although this can be challenging in the area.
- There are no trash cans, so you'll need to carry out your own trash. Remember that anything left behind will likely need to be transported by a mule.

There's no significant advantage to camping in the beginning, middle, or end, except for proximity to the falls. If you choose to camp at the end, you'll be closer to Mooney Falls, while camping at the beginning puts you nearer to Havasu Falls and the natural water spring.

9. Ensuring Food Safety

Despite my best efforts, I discovered that the squirrels and I didn't share the same understanding that human food is for humans. Hanging my food, even when it was far from the tree and strung between two trunks, proved ineffective at Havasupai.

Initially, I camped near the canyon wall and later realized that it must have been close to their habitat. It didn't take long for them to raid my food supply, leaving me with limited rations. I relocated my tent to an island and found some buckets left behind by other campers. There were also lidded buckets available, similar to those sold at Home Depot, near the front of the campsite. Using one of these buckets or bringing your own can provide an extra level of safety. Hang them or place rocks on top, as squirrels are unable to chew through plastic. Alternatively, consider bringing one of these buckets with you. I wish I had known how clever and resourceful those little creatures could be!

10. Additional Hikes: Beaver Falls, Mooney Falls, and the Colorado River

Havasu Falls is just the beginning—there's more to explore in Havasupai! Save some energy and put on your waterproof shoes, as both Beaver Falls and Mooney Falls are worth visiting on day 2 or 3. If you're up for a challenge, you can even hike all the way to the Colorado River.

Mooney Falls: You can easily reach the top of Mooney Falls by walking to the end of the campsite. While the Havasupai website advises against going beyond the campsite and displays warning signs, truthfully, reaching the bottom of Mooney Falls can be quite treacherous. The stairs become slippery and incredibly steep, with mist from the waterfall making it even more challenging. As someone who generally has a high tolerance for such situations, I personally found it to be quite precarious. Nonetheless, I would do it again.

Beaver Falls: The initial photo in this section showcases the tiered pools of Beaver Falls. This was the aspect of the trip that excited me the most, and it certainly lived up to my expectations! To reach Beaver Falls, you'll need to navigate a trail that is approximately 4 miles from Mooney Falls. The trail may not always be clearly marked, so once you descend the chain links and ladders at Mooney Falls, keep an eye out for a path on your left. Follow that path and choose the clearest and most obvious route. You'll need to cross the river multiple times, which emphasizes the importance of wearing amphibious shoes. If the weather permits, it's advisable to wear quick-drying shorts and a bathing suit for swimming. Additionally, consider using a dry bag, such as this one, to protect your camera:

Colorado River: If you begin your hike early in the morning, you can experience a side of Havasupai that few people see by hiking all the way to the confluence with the Colorado River. This hike will involve walking through water for a significant portion and will amount to approximately 16 miles round trip. If you have the time and energy, it promises to be an amazing adventure. Find more details here.

Fifty Foot Falls and Navajo Falls: Between Supai and Havasu Falls, you'll notice cascading water on your left. You can venture down to witness another set of falls, similar to Beaver Falls. These falls receive fewer visitors, and although they may have more algae, which affects the blueness of the water, they are still quite beautiful. Learn more here.

11. Photography Tips

The breathtaking baby blue color of the falls looks stunning under any lighting condition. However, I discovered that it appeared particularly captivating in diffused light, such as when there is light cloud cover. Since I visited in March and encountered some rain, the majority of the weather during my stay provided these conditions. When the sun beat down on the falls, they appeared washed out in my camera, although still breathtaking to the naked eye.

Given that we have no control over the weather, I recommend avoiding midday photography. Early mornings and late afternoons offer more favorable lighting conditions for capturing stunning photos. When I arrived at Beaver Falls around 4 pm, the lighting was perfect. Otherwise, you may encounter awkward shadows.

If you do decide to visit Beaver Falls in the afternoon, ensure that you allow sufficient time to return to the campsite before darkness falls. Remember, you'll still need to climb that precarious ladder at Mooney!

12. Drinking Water Tips

As mentioned earlier, there are no drinking water sources along the trail, so it's crucial to come prepared. Once you reach the campsite, there is a spring near the entrance where you can refill your water bottles.

Personally, I used the spring water to fill my water bottles and had no issues. However, if you're uncomfortable with this, consider bringing a filter or an alternative method for purifying your water. I personally recommend the steriPEN for spring water, but if you plan on using water from the river or near the falls, keep in mind that it may contain minerals, so a filter would be more suitable.

The farther you camp from the beginning of the campground, the farther you'll be from the clean water source. In such cases, having a filtration method is advisable.

13. Getting to the Trailhead

The nearest airports in terms of proximity are Las Vegas, which is approximately three hours away, or Phoenix. I flew into Phoenix and then drove to Flagstaff for an overnight stay before proceeding to the trailhead the next day. The entire journey from Flagstaff took about two hours.

Keep in mind that it can be extremely hot for most of the year, so it's best to reach the parking lot and begin your hike as early as possible. However, be cautious of animals on the road, and it's not advisable to drive in while it's still dark.

There are no campsites at the parking lot, but if you have a camper van or a truck, you could potentially camp there.

One of the best and closest options for an overnight stay near the parking lot and trailhead is the Hualapai Lodge. I recommend booking it immediately after obtaining your permit, as it tends to fill up quickly.

Alternatively, you can choose to start your hike later in the day and plan for an afternoon hike. However, this can be risky during hot periods, as the temperature may not have cooled down yet. Additionally, you must be confident in your hiking abilities. I began my hike around 12:30 pm and managed to arrive before the permit office closed. However, I'm uncertain of the procedures if you arrive after the permit office has closed for the day. Typically, you would present your ID for check-in and receive a wristband. There will also be staff checking cars before allowing parking.

14. Departure

When it's time to leave, remember that you'll need more time to hike back up and out than you required to come in. As the trail is generally a gradual downhill on the way in, the return hike is a gentle uphill ascent.

The earlier you can pack up and head out, the better. Alternatively, you can begin your hike in the afternoon, but ensure that you allow yourself enough time to exit before darkness falls.

I must admit, I didn't time my departure well and ended up hiking in the sun. Thankfully, it was March and there were intermittent clouds providing shade. However, I can imagine how challenging it can become during the summer!

Lastly, ensure that you have sufficient daylight to drive out, considering the presence of animals on the road as mentioned earlier.

And there you have it—an ultimate guide to Havasu Falls and everything you need to know to have a marvelous trip.

While visiting Havasu Falls requires considerable effort and financial investment, seeing the enchanting baby blue water with my own eyes made me realize that it's not just a product of Photoshop—it truly is that awe-inspiring!

Enjoy your time, capture countless memories through your camera lens, leave no trace, and have a remarkable experience!

Chapter 37: 10 Best Places To Stay In Arizona On Your Trip To The Grand Canyon State

Arizona is renowned for its stunning landscapes and captivating mountain valleys that attract numerous visitors. However, to truly experience the best of Arizona, it is essential to choose the right accommodations. The state offers a wide range of options, ensuring a perfect stay during your visit to the Grand Canyon's homeland. From luxury resorts to rustic mountain cabins, Arizona boasts a plethora of accommodations to suit every preference.

Here is a handpicked list of ten exceptional places to stay in Arizona, each offering unique characteristics that will surprise you at every turn:

1. Arizona Biltmore: This exceptional resort boasts a rich musical history and features eight swimming pools on its premises. With modern amenities such as lush gardens, luxury cabanas, exquisite dining options, and a relaxing spa, the hotel provides a truly indulgent experience. Its unique architectural design by renowned architect Frank Lloyd Wright adds to its charm. Choose from a variety of accommodations, including suites, villas, and even ocatilla.

Location: The Arizona Biltmore, 2400 East Missouri Avenue, Phoenix, Arizona, United States, 85016

2. House Boating on Lake Powell: Embark on a remarkable houseboat trip on Lake Powell and enjoy the experience of staying right on the water. This boater's paradise offers a range of exciting water sports and activities. Instead of pitching a tent, you can make your holiday unforgettable by immersing yourself in the tranquility of the lake. This makes it an ideal choice for a memorable stay in Arizona.

Location: 100 Lake Shore Dr, Page, AZ 86040, USA

3. A-Frame Mountain View Cabin in a National Forest: Nature lovers will find this property to be a paradise. Nestled in the Sonoran Desert, which is home to the iconic Saguaro cacti, this accommodation offers a unique escape from the bustling city life. Embrace the serene surroundings and indulge in activities such as mountain biking, hiking, and enjoying a BBQ grill. Disconnect from the digital world as this retreat does not provide cable or network access, allowing you to fully immerse yourself in the tranquility of nature.

Location: Flagstaff, Arizona, USA

4. Royal Palms: Situated at the base of Camelback Mountain in Phoenix, this hotel promises a classic experience enriched with luxury and modern amenities. Guests can enjoy award-winning facilities, exceptional fine dining experiences, and stunning views of nearby attractions. The adjacent restaurants further enhance the hotel's charm. It is an ideal choice for those seeking a romantic getaway in Arizona.

Location: ROYAL PALMS RESORT AND SPA, 5200 E Camelback Rd, PhoenixAZ85018

5. Jerome Grand Hotel: Located in an old mining town, this hotel is worth a visit for travelers and researchers alike. Perched at a high elevation, it offers proximity to exclusive art galleries, local restaurants, and breathtaking scenic beauty. Discover the town's fascinating history during your stay, and for those seeking a thrilling experience, embark on a ghost hunting adventure at this haunted hotel.

Location: P. O. Box H, 200 Hill Street, Jerome, Arizona 86331

6. Hotel Congress: Known for its captivating stories and vibrant atmosphere, this hotel has long been an attraction for travelers. Today, it stands as one of the best places to stay in Arizona. With a blend of urban and vintage decor, the hotel showcases exclusive murals adorning its walls. The property is also home to Club Congress and Tiger's Tap Room, offering exciting entertainment options.

Location: 311 East Congress Street, Tucson, AZ 85701 USA

7. The Shady Dell: For a unique vintage experience, choose to stay in one of the aluminum trailers at The Shady Dell. Each trailer comes with its own lawn and stylish interior decoration, featuring leopard print carpets. Enjoy excellent dining options and a comfortable stay in this nostalgic setting. It is undoubtedly one of the best choices for a memorable stay in Arizona.

Location: The Shady Dell Vintage Trailer Court, 1 Old Douglas Road, Bisbee, AZ 85603

8. Moxy: This innovative hotel stands out for its art, culture, and music scene, thanks to its proximity to the ASU campus. Guests can enjoy live performances by local artists and partake in the hotel's unique yoga series. Each room is equipped with guitars and record players, adding a touch of creativity to your stay.

Location: 1333 S Rural Rd, Tempe, AZ 85281, USA

9. The Grand Canyon Motel: Offering a truly exceptional experience, this hotel transforms train carts into stylish rooms. Combining vintage charm with modern amenities, it is located in a prime location, allowing you to explore the area's natural beauty. Enjoy the best of both worlds during your stay at this historic cottage.

Location: 317 South State Route 64, Valle, AZ

10. Wigwam Motel: This listed property exudes eternal vintage charm and rich history. Surrounded by roadside landmarks, the motel offers comfortable accommodations with modern amenities and exclusive dining experiences, providing a truly memorable stay.

Location: 811 W Hopi Dr, Holbrook, AZ 86025, USA

These ten remarkable places represent the finest accommodations in Arizona, ensuring an unforgettable experience in this remarkable state.

Chapter 38: Benefits of Sustainable Tourism & How to Travel Responsibly

You've probably heard about sustainable travel and the rise of green tourism in recent years. While travel can be enjoyable and eye-opening, it can also harm the environment and local communities if not done responsibly. Unfortunately, not all travelers make well-informed decisions that prioritize the best interests of their destinations.

That's why sustainable tourism should be more than an afterthought – it should be the norm. To help you travel more responsibly, we're here to guide you through the benefits of eco-tourism and how you can make a positive difference.

We'll explain what sustainable tourism is and discuss its benefits for you, local communities, and the environment, so you can make informed decisions about your future trips!

What is sustainable tourism?
Sustainable tourism involves traveling with the purpose of creating a positive impact on the environment, society, and economy.

It means minimizing negative impacts on the places you visit and contributing to the overall development and conservation of travel destinations. This includes protecting the environment and the welfare of the people who depend on it.

So, is tourism truly sustainable?
While there are many ways to travel responsibly, it's important to acknowledge that tourism can never be completely sustainable. Like any industry, it has its own impact.

As a traveler, you can help shift the tourism industry towards sustainability by making conscious choices that ensure the environment and local communities can thrive.

Whether you're preparing to study in South Africa, intern in England, or volunteer in Thailand, there are numerous ways to make your travel more sustainable. By practicing eco-friendly, responsible travel and understanding the benefits of sustainable tourism, you can leave a positive impact.

Benefits of sustainable tourism
Now that you understand the impact of green tourism on the places you visit, let's explore some of the incredible benefits of eco-tourism.

1. IT HAS A LOWER ECOLOGICAL IMPACT
Every action you take during your vacation has an ecological footprint – how you get there, where you stay, the activities you participate in, and even the food you eat. The goal of green tourism is to minimize this impact.

While travel should be relaxing, there are simple ways to protect the environment during your trip. Choosing to eat local produce and support local businesses can make a significant difference. Imported food, whether from other regions or countries, comes at a high economic and environmental cost. Exploring new places through local cuisine not only reduces emissions but also introduces you to exciting flavors you may fall in love with.

To further reduce your carbon footprint, consider alternative travel methods such as trains, buses, or other eco-friendly options when your destination is accessible by land. When air travel is necessary, opt for direct flights and consider purchasing carbon offsets. And don't forget to pack lightly!

2. IT ALLOWS WILDLIFE TO THRIVE IN THEIR NATURAL HABITAT

Preserving wildlife is a crucial aspect of responsible tourism. In many destinations, animals are exploited to attract tourists, leading to their mistreatment.

Activities like riding elephants in Thailand or swimming with pink dolphins in the Amazon may seem innocent, but they harm these animals. Elephants suffer from pain and early deaths, while dolphins are lured by frozen fish supplied by tourism providers. Tourists engage in activities that involve touching, riding, and restraining these animals, often for photo opportunities. Some even take parts of the animals as souvenirs, such as tortoise shells, tiger fangs, or ivory.

Making informed travel decisions allows you to avoid attractions that prioritize entertainment over animal welfare. By reducing the demand for such activities, we can eventually eliminate them. This shift empowers local communities to engage in sustainable travel jobs, protect wildlife, and embrace green tourism instead of exploitation.

If you truly want to experience wildlife up close, consider volunteering for conservation projects. Adding a volunteering period to your trip offers an unforgettable experience while supporting important initiatives and reaping the benefits of sustainable tourism.

3. RESPONSIBLE TOURISM MAINTAINS CLEAN ENVIRONMENTS

It's easy to overlook environmental cleanliness while exploring local markets or relaxing at resorts. However, this negligence often leads to excessive waste, from plastic pollution on beaches to excessive energy consumption in hotels.

Green tourism starts with responsible choices. When researching accommodations, look for signs of environmental responsibility, such as proper waste management and sustainable practices. Be critical of greenwashing – ensure that hotels' eco claims are backed by tangible actions. Ask about their reduction of single-use plastics, their waste management strategies, and their efforts to conserve energy and water.

Opting for sustainable travel destinations rather than overcrowded places suffering from the negative impacts of mass tourism also helps protect the environment.

When packing for your trip, consider bringing eco-conscious items that reduce waste, such as reusable cutlery, food containers, straws, and water bottles. Cloth napkins, a toiletry bag with reusable travel-sized containers, and a travel towel are also helpful. Menstrual cups, reusable shopping bags or backpacks, and other sustainable choices contribute to cleaner communities and the preservation of the places you visit.

4. IT SUPPORTS AND EMPOWERS LOCAL COMMUNITIES

By supporting local communities, you have the opportunity to immerse yourself in their culture.

Choosing locally owned hotels, guesthouses, and homestays directly stimulates the local economy and allows you to connect with locals on a personal level. Reputable local tour operators provide similar experiences while employing locals in sustainable travel jobs and ensuring that your holiday budget benefits the people who made your trip memorable.

Eating at local restaurants offers a chance to savor authentic, healthy, and reasonably priced food, as ingredients are sourced locally. Shopping for local products and souvenirs allows you to buy unique items while supporting local artisans.

5. IT PRESERVES CULTURAL HERITAGE

When done responsibly, tourism provides opportunities for educational and insightful experiences, encouraging locals to share their cultural heritage.

Traveling with a focus on cultural richness, such as through a gap year program, allows you to learn traditional crafts from local artisans – an experience you can't replicate elsewhere.

Promoting cultural heritage instills pride in locals, encouraging them to preserve their traditions and develop sustainable travel destinations.

In conclusion, sustainable tourism is about making conscious choices to create a positive impact on the environment, society, and economy. By practicing eco-friendly travel, supporting local communities, and preserving cultural heritage, you can enjoy your trips while leaving a lasting, positive legacy.

6. YOU'LL HAVE A MORE MEANINGFUL EXPERIENCE

Imagine crossing the desert off your bucket list. You rent a 4x4 and drive across the dunes, ending the day with a picturesque picnic overlooking the vast expanse of sand. It's a remarkable sight that leaves you in awe.

But if you choose to stay with the nomadic Bedouins during your trip, you'll gain a glimpse into their traditional desert-dwelling lifestyle. You'll witness firsthand how they navigate the challenging landscapes, immerse yourself in their music and poetry, and be embraced by their incredible hospitality.

Engaging in green tourism opens doors to more than just the beauty of the places you visit. It offers the opportunity for a deeper, more meaningful connection with the communities you encounter, leaving you with lasting memories and a greater understanding of diverse cultures.

7. YOU BECOME A MORE CONSCIOUS TRAVELER

One of the greatest benefits of sustainable tourism is developing a heightened sense of responsibility in your travel choices.

This could involve opting for greener transportation methods to reach your destination and selecting eco-conscious accommodations.

You may also discover that certain locations are not conducive to sustainability. Some small islands struggle to support an influx of tourists, and communities may lack the infrastructure to accommodate large numbers of visitors. In these cases, it's best to avoid such destinations altogether.

Other ways to engage in responsible tourism include dining at local restaurants instead of bringing fast food back to your hotel, supporting important causes during your vacation time, and embracing a slower travel pace to truly appreciate and respect the places you visit.

Responsible travel tips:
- Choose sustainable travel destinations, venture off the beaten path, or visit during the off-season.
- Embrace slow travel. Rather than rushing to check off all the top tourist attractions, spend more time exploring a country, allowing yourself to fully immerse in the local environment and connect with the people. This provides a deeper understanding of the culture, history, and traditions.
- Conserve energy by turning off lights and unplugging electronic devices when not in use.

- Take shorter showers and do laundry in larger loads to minimize water usage.
- Reuse towels and bed linen unless they are soiled.
- Dress respectfully and appropriately for the destinations you plan to visit.
- Always ask for permission before taking photos of locals.
- Learn a few basic phrases in the local language to foster connections with the community.
- When posting on social media, be mindful of geotagging pristine and untouched landscapes to avoid contributing to mass tourism.
- In fragile ecosystems, ensure that the area is properly maintained and learn about local conservation efforts.
- Choose accommodations that employ and treat locals well, with bonus points for promoting diversity and inclusivity.
- Support tourism businesses that comply with local regulations and possess sustainable credentials.
- Inquire about the environmental policies of the accommodations and services you book, and choose those committed to sustainability.

Chapter 39: The Ultimate Arizona Road Trip Itinerary

On this itinerary for an Arizona road trip, you'll have the opportunity to explore three national parks, witness the stunning landscapes of Monument Valley, stroll through the enchanting Antelope Canyon, and hike the desert hills of Sedona. Arizona is renowned for its iconic natural scenery, and this road trip allows you to experience it all.

Given the vastness of Arizona and the multitude of attractions, be prepared for a busy schedule. However, the adventure will be well worth it. Witness the sunrise at Horseshoe Bend, embark on enjoyable short hikes in Sedona, encounter an abundance of cacti in Saguaro National Park, explore the unique landscapes of Petrified Forest, and witness the sunset over the Grand Canyon.

This 10-day itinerary is designed to provide a comprehensive experience. However, if you have less time available, we'll provide recommendations on how to condense the itinerary at the end of this chapter. Conversely, if you have more time, there are additional destinations we can suggest.

During this Arizona road trip, you'll visit the following locations:
- Saguaro National Park
- Petrified Forest National Park
- Grand Canyon National Park
- Sedona
- Monument Valley
- Antelope Canyon
- Horseshoe Bend
- Valley of the Gods (optional)

Arizona Road Trip Itinerary:
Day 1: Arrive in Phoenix, Visit Saguaro National Park
Day 2: Explore Saguaro National Park
Day 3: Discover Petrified Forest National Park
Day 4: Experience Monument Valley
Day 5: Visit Antelope Canyon
Day 6-7: Explore the Grand Canyon
Day 8: Continue Exploring the Grand Canyon and Proceed to Sedona
Day 9: Enjoy Sedona
Day 10: Departure

Arizona Itinerary: Day 1
Arrive in Phoenix, Visit Saguaro National Park

Travel time: 2-3 hours (110-160 miles)

To maximize your day, aim to arrive in Phoenix by midday. This will allow you to drive to Saguaro National Park in Tucson in the afternoon, and even explore parts of the park if time permits.

The journey from Phoenix to Tucson takes slightly over an hour and a half. If you choose to visit one section of Saguaro National Park, it will involve some additional driving, but this means you'll have less driving to do the following day.

Saguaro National Park derives its name from the Saguaro cactus, which exclusively grows in the Sonoran Desert.

The park consists of two separate sections, with the city of Tucson situated between them. The Rincon Mountain District, located in the east, boasts a picturesque backdrop provided by the Rincon Mountains, although it features a lower concentration of cacti. The Tucson Mountain District, in the west, is more popular due to its higher density of cacti.

If you arrive in the early to mid-afternoon, you'll have sufficient time to explore the Rincon Mountain District. There's a short scenic drive available, with the option to embark on a few easy trails.

Recommended Accommodations in Tucson:
- Upscale: JW Marriott Tucson Starr Pass Resort and Spa, an excellent resort offering swimming pools, restaurants, outdoor activities, and a convenient location close to Saguaro West.
- Mid-Range: Cactus Cove Bed and Breakfast Inn, an adult-only bed and breakfast situated in eastern Tucson, near Saguaro East. The property features an outdoor pool and stunning mountain views.
- Budget: Hotel McCoy, conveniently located just off Route 10. This hotel offers a 30-minute drive to both Saguaro West and Saguaro East. Guests can enjoy the pool and locally produced beer, wine, and coffee.

Arizona Itinerary: Day 2
Explore Saguaro National Park

Travel time: 4.5 hours (240 miles)

Spend the day exploring Saguaro National Park, then in the late afternoon or early evening, make your way to Petrified Forest National Park.

If you had the opportunity to visit the east section of Saguaro National Park on the previous afternoon, you'll have ample time to explore the west section today. Most likely, you'll finish your visit by midday, allowing for a comfortable drive to Petrified Forest National Park.

This day involves one of the longer drives of the Arizona road trip. The journey from Tucson to Petrified Forest takes you through remote desert landscapes.

In the evening, stay in Holbrook, the nearest town to Petrified Forest National Park.

Recommended Accommodations in Holbrook:
- Brad's Desert Inn, a quirky motel located right on historic Route 66, offering plenty of character.
- Days Inn, a comfortable and quiet option with decent Wi-Fi, ideal for a restful stay during your visit.
- La Quinta Inn & Suites, a highly rated hotel with excellent family-friendly options, accommodating over five people in their suites.

Arizona Itinerary: Day 3
Discover Petrified Forest National Park

Travel time: 5 hours (280 miles)

Dedicate the day to exploring Petrified Forest National Park before continuing north to Monument Valley.

Similar to Saguaro, Petrified Forest is a relatively small park that can be fully experienced in one day or less.

The park consists of two sections. The northern half showcases the vibrant hills of the Painted Desert, offering stunning photography opportunities and short hikes through the backcountry. The southern section is renowned for its petrified wood, ancient logs dating back millions of years.

In the mid-afternoon, hit the road again and drive north to Monument Valley. While it's another day of significant driving, the subsequent drives for the remainder of the Arizona road trip will be shorter. The journey from Holbrook to Monument Valley takes approximately three and a half hours.

Recommended Accommodations in Monument Valley:
- The View Hotel, located within Monument Valley Tribal Park. Choose between hotel rooms or cabins, both offering breathtaking views. The cabins feature decks overlooking the Mittens, allowing you to enjoy the scenery right from your bed.
- Goulding's Lodge and Campground, situated just outside Monument Valley Tribal Park. The lodge provides rooms with stunning views, and they also offer a campground. They operate one of the few restaurants in the area.
- Firetree B&B is another nearby bed and breakfast option worth considering.

Arizona Itinerary: Day 4
Experience Monument Valley

Minimal travel required; if visiting Valley of the Gods in Utah, drive for 2 hours (72 miles)

Devote the entire day to exploring Monument Valley. While it may seem like a lot of time, there is plenty to do and see in this captivating destination. Additionally, if you have a hotel or cabin with a view, it's an ideal place to relax and unwind before continuing your journey.

In Monument Valley, take the 17-mile Valley Drive loop, which offers stunning views of the most popular sites. Other recommended experiences include visiting Forrest Gump Point, embarking on a guided tour of

Monument Valley, and optionally detouring to the Valley of the Gods. Don't forget to catch the sunset over the Mittens.

Note that certain sections of Monument Valley can only be accessed via guided tours, as they are located on Navajo land. However, these tours are well worth it. Choose from sunrise or sunset photography tours, explore petroglyphs and Anasazi sites,

Spend the night in Monument Valley.

Arizona Itinerary: Day 5
Antelope Canyon

Travel time: 2 hours (120 miles)

Begin your day early to allow ample time for a tour of Antelope Canyon.

Antelope Canyon consists of two slot canyons, namely Upper Antelope Canyon and Lower Antelope Canyon. Since they are located on Navajo lands, access is restricted to guided tours.

Arriving by 10 am will provide sufficient time to explore both canyons. Upper Antelope Canyon, with its unique light beams, shifting sands, and towering canyon walls, is particularly renowned for its photogenic qualities.

Lower Antelope Canyon offers a more adventurous experience, with narrow passageways to navigate and ladders to climb. Many visitors find it to be a more enjoyable option. However, be prepared for crowds, as this destination has become increasingly popular in recent years.

Pro Travel Tip: Make reservations well in advance, ideally 4 to 6 months ahead, especially during the summer season. Tickets can also be purchased through GetYourGuide.

In the evening, make sure to visit Horseshoe Bend to witness the stunning sunset. Keep in mind that this location is also quite popular, so arrive early if you want an unobstructed view from the rim.

Recommended Accommodations in Page:
- Holiday Inn Express: A clean, convenient, and budget-friendly option.
- Wingate by Wyndham Page Lake Powell: Highly rated hotel in Page.
- Hyatt Place Page Lake Powell: Another well-regarded choice for accommodations.

Arizona Itinerary: Day 6
Grand Canyon

Travel time: 2.5 hours (135 miles)

In the morning, you have the option to witness the sunrise at Horseshoe Bend. During this time, the crowds are lighter, providing a peaceful and serene atmosphere. It offers a distinct experience compared to the bustling sunset views on busy evenings.

Proceed to the Grand Canyon by entering through the east entrance.

While driving along Desert View Drive, you'll encounter numerous viewpoints as you make your way to the Grand Canyon Village. Each of these viewpoints is breathtaking, but our favorites include Desert View Point (along with the Desert View Watchtower), Moran Point, and Grand View Point.

Check into your hotel and spend the afternoon exploring more viewpoints along the South Rim. You can opt to walk the South Rim Trail, utilize the shuttle service, or even bike to take in the panoramic vistas. End the day by watching the sunset over the Grand Canyon and enjoying dinner.

Recommended Accommodations at the Grand Canyon:

- El Tovar, Thunderbird Lodge, Bright Angel Lodge, Kachina Lodge, and Maswick Lodge are five hotels situated in the Grand Canyon Village. Staying here allows for easy access to shuttles, short walks to various viewpoints, and eliminates the hassle of driving in and out of the park. However, keep in mind that these hotels receive mixed reviews and can be considered expensive for the value provided.

Alternatively, you have the option to stay in Tusayan, which is a 15-minute drive from the park. There are several hotels available, as well as various restaurants.

The Grand Hotel in Tusayan is highly recommended, with impressive exteriors and a lovely lobby. However, the rooms are considered average. The hotel is listed as a 5-star establishment on Booking.com, but it may feel more like a 3 to 4-star hotel. Consider upgrading to a Deluxe Queen Room for a more pleasant stay.

Other hotels to consider in Tusayan include Best Western and Holiday Inn Express.

You will spend two nights in the area.

Arizona Itinerary: Day 7
Grand Canyon

Minimal travel required

With a full day at the Grand Canyon, there are numerous ways to make the most of your time.

For avid hikers, we recommend the South Kaibab Trail, which offers unbelievable views and tends to be less crowded compared to the more famous (yet less scenic, in our opinion) Bright Angel Trail. You can choose to hike to Cedar Ridge or Skeleton Point and then return.

For an epic experience, consider hiking from the South Rim to the North Rim via the South Kaibab and Bright Angel Trails. This challenging trek is only recommended during the cooler months (November through March) and is suitable for experienced hikers in excellent physical condition.

Even if hiking isn't your primary interest, a hike to Ooh Aah Point on the South Kaibab Trail is a memorable experience, particularly in the early morning.

Other activities to consider include a helicopter flight over the Grand Canyon, a visit to the Yavapai Museum of Geology, a bike ride along Hermit Road, or watching the Grand Canyon IMAX movie.

Retire for the night within the Grand Canyon area.

Day 9: Sedona
Midday: Enjoy lunch in Sedona. In the early afternoon, embark on a thrilling 4WD road tour of Broken Arrow, the most exciting off-road adventure in Sedona.

Late afternoon: Set out on a hike to Devils Bridge, the most popular trail in Sedona. From 8 am to 4 pm, the trail tends to be extremely busy. However, by 3:30 pm, most visitors are heading back, making this the ideal time to hike to Devils Bridge. Not only will you encounter fewer crowds, but the lighting conditions will be perfect for photography.

Evening: Treat yourself to dinner at one of Sedona's excellent restaurants. Mariposa, Vino di Sedona, Saltrock Southwest Kitchen, and Elote Café are some of our favorites. Be sure to make reservations in advance.

If you're not keen on hiking, here's an alternative itinerary for the day:

Morning: Indulge in a delicious brunch at The Coffee Pot Restaurant, Wildflower, or Miley's Café (located in the Village of Oak Creek). Follow it up with a visit to the Tlaquepaque Arts and Crafts Village for some shopping. You can have lunch at Tlaquepaque or The Hudson.

Midday: Explore the Chapel of the Holy Cross, a small Roman Catholic church perched on the red rocks. For a unique and tranquil experience, visit the Amitabha Stupa and Peace Park. Spend the rest of the afternoon at Crescent Moon Picnic Site, where you can capture iconic views of Cathedral Rock. Another option is to join a small group tour by Jeep to discover the Sedona vortexes.

Evening: Enjoy a delightful dinner in Sedona. You can choose to spend the night in Sedona or drive to Phoenix if you have an early flight tomorrow.

Arizona Itinerary: Day 10
Fly Home

On the road: 2 hours (120 miles)

Today, it's time to either fly home or continue your onward journey.

Best Time for This Arizona Road Trip
This road trip can be undertaken year-round.

The optimal months are from March to May and late September to mid-November when the weather is pleasant and the parks are less crowded.

During the summer months (June to August), expect scorching temperatures and larger crowds.

Winter months may bring snow, particularly around the Grand Canyon, which can affect travel. However, if you don't mind the cold weather and the possibility of snow, this is a quieter time to visit the area.

We have personally visited in May, June, and December, with May being our favorite time followed closely by December.

How to Modify This Itinerary

With More Time:
Visit the North Rim of the Grand Canyon:
You can make a day trip from Page or spend the night there. Keep in mind that if you choose to spend the night, the drive to the South Rim of the Grand Canyon on the following day will be quite long.

The North Rim offers spectacular views of the Grand Canyon, although there are fewer activities compared to the South Rim. Half a day is usually sufficient to explore this area.

Please note that the North Rim is open only from mid-May to mid-October.

Vermilion Cliffs National Monument:
You can add an extra day to your itinerary to go hiking in this area. If you're seeking an awe-inspiring destination in Arizona, look no further than Vermilion Cliffs National Monument. Nestled in the northern part of the state, this captivating monument offers a breathtaking tapestry of vibrant colors, towering cliffs, and unique geological formations that will leave you enchanted. Vermilion Cliffs National Monument spans over 280,000 acres of pristine wilderness, providing a sanctuary for rare plants, diverse wildlife, and stunning natural wonders.

The Wave:
The Wave: One of the most iconic and sought-after attractions within the monument is The Wave. This extraordinary sandstone formation showcases mesmerizing, swirling patterns and hues. Due to its popularity, access is limited, and a permit is required. Planning ahead and securing a permit will allow you to witness this natural masterpiece up close.

Canyon de Chelly National Monument:
Located in northeast Arizona on Navajo tribal lands, Canyon de Chelly National Monument is an intriguing national monument that's not far from Monument Valley.

With Less Time:
To create a 9-day itinerary, remove one day from the Grand Canyon.

For an 8-day itinerary, consider excluding Saguaro National Park. Saguaro involves additional driving, and in our opinion, the other destinations on this list offer more captivating experiences.

To make it a 7-day itinerary, reduce your time in Monument Valley.

7-Day Arizona Road Trip Itinerary:
Day 1: Arrive in Phoenix, drive to Petrified Forest National Park.
Day 2: Petrified Forest National Park, drive to Monument Valley.
Day 3: Monument Valley, drive to Page.
Day 4: Antelope Canyon, drive to the Grand Canyon.
Day 5: Grand Canyon National Park.
Day 6: Drive to Sedona, explore Sedona.
Day 7: Fly home.

Practical Information:
National Park Fees:
- Saguaro NP: $25.
- Petrified Forest NP: $25.
- Grand Canyon NP: $35.
Total: $85.

America the Beautiful Pass:
Consider purchasing the America the Beautiful Pass if you plan to visit Saguaro, Petrified Forest, and Grand Canyon National Parks. This annual

pass costs $80 and grants access to the parks for one year. It also provides free admission to other national parks and federal recreation sites visited within 365 days of purchasing the pass. You can buy the pass at the first national park you visit or online.

Printed in Great Britain
by Amazon